"Any campus ministry passionate about students' lives being transformed will want this book in the hands of their front-line campus staff. Steve Smallman has renewed my own biblical understanding of God's prior work in the hearts of 'not yet believers' while inspiring me to embrace my role as a spiritual midwife in the lives of college students."

    —**Bruce Alwood**, Team Member, World Harvest Mission (now Serge)

"*Beginnings* transforms that most dangerous journey—one's spiritual pilgrimage—into safe, known territory. By applying a pastor's heart and a willing ear to hundreds of testimonies heard over decades of ministry, Stephen Smallman has distilled the work of God in the soul: 'When God calls, we come.' In place of our too-often clichéd born-again narratives, he guides us to a richer understanding that is wonderfully profound and reassuringly practical."

    —**Mindy Belz**, Editor, *WORLD*

" 'Born again' is a common expression that few people understand. In a compelling way Stephen Smallman helps us understand that it is the supernatural work of the Holy Spirit. This book will prove profitable to all who read it."

    —**Jerry Bridges**, Author, *The Pursuit of Holiness*

"I believe this book will be profoundly helpful for youth workers or anyone sharing the gospel. Becoming a Christian is a process, not just a onetime conversion event. Steve Smallman biblically maps out this spiritual birth process. Too often Christian workers are frustrated with 'new converts' because they do not seem to be growing fast enough. The truth is that many 'new converts' may profess with their mouths that they are believers in Jesus Christ, but their hearts and minds are still trying to process the gospel. Smallman helps us understand the process of this miraculous and mysterious work of the Holy Spirit of bringing people into the kingdom of God. Smallman makes it very clear that in order for the gospel message to be believed, 'it requires a powerful moving of God to make the gospel message come alive to a listener.' *Beginnings* is a biblically based work on understanding the process of becoming a Christian."

—**Brian Fletcher**, Associate Pastor, Spring Run Presbyterian

"Having read *Beginnings* I found myself reinterpreting the way God has put his hand on my life since I was a small boy. It filled me with thankfulness to God for his sovereign work and gave me an interpretive framework of new birth that was not only more accurate, all-embracing, and truthful, but, more importantly, God-centered. This has been an immensely helpful addition to my evangelistic thinking and training as an evangelist in a local church seeking to 'prepare God's people for works of service' (Eph. 4) as witnesses for Christ. Understanding the birthline tool will keep us in awe of what God does in the lives of individuals and turn us from salesmen to midwives."

—**Rico Tice**, Founder, Christianity Explored

"Steve Smallman's stories of how God brings people to new life in Christ are exhilarating—and his refreshing insights into the process of conversion are also immensely encouraging to anyone who wants to share his or her faith."

—**Ellen Vaughn**, Author, *Radical Gratitude*

"*Beginnings* has proven to be one of the best-loved and most important books in our program. It is one of the books that we have our fellows read as they consider the themes of grace and true conversion and spend time writing their own spiritual autobiography in preparation for our retreat. We are so thankful for such a helpful book."

—**Joel S. Woodruff**, Vice President of Discipleship and Outreach, C. S. Lewis Institute

Beginnings

Beginnings

UNDERSTANDING HOW WE EXPERIENCE
THE NEW BIRTH

STEPHEN SMALLMAN

P&R PUBLISHING
P.O. BOX 817 • PHILLIPSBURG • NEW JERSEY 08865-0817

ISBN: 978-1-59638-945-8 (pbk)
ISBN: 978-1-59638-946-5 (ePub)
ISBN: 978-1-59638-947-2 (Mobi)

Printed in the United States of America

Library of Congress Cataloging-in-Publication Data

Smallman, Stephen, 1940-
  [Spiritual birthline]
  Beginnings : understanding how we experience the new birth / Stephen Smallman.
     pages cm
  Includes bibliographical references and index.
   ISBN 978-1-59638-945-8 (pbk.) -- ISBN 978-1-59638-946-5 (ePub) -- ISBN 978-1-59638-947-2 (Mobi)
  1. Conversion--Christianity. I. Title.
  BR110.S62 2015
  248.2'4--dc23
                                    2014036612

To Sandy,
my wife, friend,
and faithful partner in over forty years of ministry

Contents

CONTENTS

Foreword

ONE OF THE MOST CRUCIAL challenges facing the evangelical church today is that so many of those who fill our churches and profess to follow Christ have not truly experienced the transforming work of the Holy Spirit in new birth.

In my book *Being the Body*, I devote a chapter to explaining this phenomenon, which I refer to as "The Sin of Presumption." The presumption is that leading someone to pray a prayer or come forward in a revival meeting transforms him into a "born-again Christian." (Conversely, there are people whose lives give clear evidence of their love for Christ and devoted service to him but who haven't undergone the classic conversion experience that is the stuff of testimonies. Because they lack this experience, others question the genuineness of their salvation. This, too, is presumption.)

Unless we understand true conversion in terms of the work of the Spirit, we will continue this sin of presumption, and nominal Christians will continue to fill our pews. As I wrote in *Being the Body*:

> New life in the Spirit is conceived in the secret place of the soul, hidden from human eyes. This is the wonder and mystery

9

of God's regeneration of men and women. And never in this life will we quite know how God calls His people to Himself. What we do know is that *the wind of the Spirit blows where He wills.* We hear the sound, we see the evidence, but we cannot comprehend fully how this mysterious breath of God touches human hearts. God builds His church in the most unlikely ways and places, stirring the convictions of the heart, bringing men and women to the knowledge of sin, to repentance, to the Savior Himself—and knitting them together in His body.[1]

My friend Steve Smallman has written an important book that explains the link between the work of the Spirit and the conversion experience. The book contains substantial theological and biblical understanding, but Steve has written as a pastor with years of experience in working with people. His goal is to help Christians understand their own experience and in turn become spiritual midwives, helping others come to Christ in a way that is sensitive to the mysterious working of the Spirit.

Steve was serving as the pastor of McLean (Virginia) Presbyterian Church during the time of my own conversion. Because Patty and I were living in McLean and the offices of Prison Fellowship were first located there, a substantial number of our staff attended Steve's church. Thus it's not surprising that a great deal of the material for this book grew out of Steve's involvement with us in those early days of our ministry. He was one of our first seminar leaders, and he used his *Birthline* teaching both in prisons and during his ministry with prisoners we brought to Washington. I have appreciated Steve's teach-

1. Charles Colson and Ellen Vaughn, *Being the Body* (Nashville: W Publishing Group, 2003), 58.

ing, preaching, and leadership and value his insights into my own experience.

The Spirit is still moving, like the blowing of the wind, in the hearts of men, women, and children all over the world. We humans enjoy the extraordinary privilege of playing a part in what the Spirit is doing. May the Lord help us to be involved in this great work, but never presume that we can accomplish what only the Spirit is capable of.

CHARLES W. COLSON
March 2005

Preface

The wind blows wherever it pleases. You hear its sound, but you cannot tell where it comes from or where it is going. So it is with everyone born of the Spirit. (Jesus, in John 3:8)

THIS IS A BOOK ABOUT people personally experiencing the work of the Holy Spirit in spiritual birth. I readily acknowledge that this is not an easy topic to write about accurately. Jesus described the new birth as mysterious as the coming and going of the wind. On the one hand there are biblical and theological studies about the work of the Holy Spirit; on the other hand are discussions of conversion and conversion experiences. But can the two themes be brought together in a way that is of practical value to multitudes of people who are on the "front lines" encountering the mysterious work of God every day in the lives of ordinary people—themselves and others? That is what I have attempted to do in this book. Whether or not I succeed I will leave up to you, the reader.

The original edition of this book appeared under the title, *Spiritual Birthline: Understanding How We Experience the New Birth.* I was very honored that Charles Colson agreed to write the foreword and that he supported my understanding of his coming to faith (chapter 6). Chuck was called to be with his Savior in 2012, and I want to add my voice to the thousands who have expressed appreciation for his godly example and leadership.

This is a very personal book. I include a number of stories, and some have asked why I didn't include my own. This whole book is my story. It is a result of my quest to understand how God called me to himself as a teenager with no church or religious background. I experienced a dramatic conversion when I walked the "sawdust trail" at a revival meeting. I assumed, as do so many, that my experience was the norm. But then I began to raise children in a very different environment than I had known. I was also a pastor of the same congregation for thirty years and watched many whose struggle to believe was not the same as mine. For a season I was very involved with men and women in prisons, and I regularly heard and evaluated their stories.

Just as important as those observations has been the extraordinary privilege of intensely studying Scripture to prepare for sermons and lessons over decades of ministry. Scripture is the "double-edged sword" (Heb. 4:12) that cuts into the very core of a person and lays bare the soul. It has done that to me, but I have also seen how others were changed by the Word of God.

The stories I include are personal. In almost every instance they are about people I know or have come from people I know. As I say in the book, every person who has been born again has a story to tell. So there is no end to the resource material available. But I wanted to pass along stories that I knew to be authentic. In most instances these are people I still know and who verified the information and gave me permission to include their stories, including their names. In a few instances it has been appropriate to change the names or some of the circumstances, but it was still information that I could confirm as factual. I think I have asked people on every continent and from all sorts of backgrounds to tell me the stories of God's work in their new birth. In addition I have received dozens of case studies from students. Even though just a fraction of these stories are told, I hope they represent a fair sampling of the gracious work of God in all kinds of people, in all kinds of circumstances.

In 2009 P&R Publishing printed *The Walk*, a book written for "new and renewed followers of Jesus." I deliberately wrote it as a "dummies-style" introduction to discipleship and attempted to speak directly to those with very little background in the faith. I'm pleased that many have found it to be a very useful resource in helping seekers as well as believers follow Christ as "beginners." This book, which we have titled *Beginnings*, is a companion to *The Walk* and should be used as a leaders' guide for those actively involved in making disciples, including both leading people to faith and then nurturing them in the faith. The approaches to ministry are complementary. The one significant addition to *Beginnings* is a case study from my friend, Doug Logan, pastor of Epiphany Fellowship in Camden, New Jersey. Doug also wrote a very thoughtful essay about how the approach of this book has had a direct impact on reaching into his community. It is an appendix and should be read as an example of how to apply the birthline idea in general ministry, not just to see how it applies to the unique challenges of his community.

I am very grateful that P&R Publishing felt the book was important enough to keep in print. I have enjoyed working with Amanda Martin. The book is essentially unchanged from the original, but I have added a few footnotes with some of the current literature that has appeared since 2006 and have updated some of the case studies.

I am grateful to my four children for their encouragement and their willingness to "honor their father and mother" as they have put their stories into writing. We are very blessed to have such children.

Sandy, my wife, is my main sounding board and my primary editor. Not much that I write is passed along until she has reviewed and corrected it. I don't know what I would have done without her support and encouragement. She has stood by me "in plenty and in want; in joy and in sorrow," and I thank God for her.

CHAPTER 1

Kathy's Story

KATHY WAS A YOUNG WOMAN who lived the good life that the Washington, DC, of the 1990s offered an upwardly mobile woman who was attractive and well educated. She was a successful stockbroker who dressed well, drove a good car, and kept herself in excellent shape for running marathons. Kathy was also living with a man who had promised to marry her when the time was right.

This beautiful life started to crumble when her fiancé announced that he was gay and decided to stop trying to live a straight life. It took a further hit when several months later he called Kathy to tell her that he had just been diagnosed with the HIV virus and urged her to get herself checked. At that early point AIDS was considered to be exclusively a disease of gay men and drug addicts, so Kathy ignored his warnings. However, after several more months she began to notice that she was finding it difficult to get into shape for her next marathon, and she was having a harder and harder time concentrating at work. This went on until she could no longer put off a visit to the doctor.

It was then that she found out that not only did she have the HIV virus, but it had grown into full-blown AIDS. She walked out of the doctor's office having heard her death sentence.

One of the first things Kathy determined she needed to do was to talk to her boss. He was a man she respected, so she was comfortable telling him her exact situation. On hearing her story Carl asked if she would be offended if he set aside business for a moment and talked to her personally. When she expressed her willingness to do this, Carl asked how this was affecting her spiritually. Kathy spoke of a Roman Catholic upbringing from which she had turned away as an adult. She then listened as Carl spoke briefly of his own spiritual journey and the church he and his wife had recently found. He invited Kathy to attend with him and his wife.

A few weeks later Kathy accepted Carl's invitation and met him and his family at the church, where she insisted on sitting in the back row. But she came back the next week and the next, and even accepted an invitation to attend a Sunday evening gathering of singles. She decided to be frank with them about her situation just as she had been with Carl, and to her surprise and delight they accepted and loved her. Kathy became a regular both Sunday morning and evening, even though she still didn't think of herself as religious.

I became involved in Kathy's story in September 1991. I was returning from a nine-month sabbatical and decided to resume my preaching ministry with a series of messages entitled "Meet Your New Pastor." This seemed to fit because I was personally renewed by my time away (my first significant break after more than twenty years of pastoring the church), and I also knew that a number of people had started attending since I left. For the first message I told the story of my coming to faith as a teenager with no church background at all. At the end of the message I spoke of coming to Christ in very much the same way that a baby is born. A seed of life is planted by God, but it has to grow, very much like a pregnancy. Finally that new life "goes public," and just like a newborn baby, there is a cry as we confess Christ. I described how I had done that in my conversion experience. I then explained that while not everyone has the same experience, when the time is right to give ourselves to Christ we know it. I had no idea at the time that Kathy was sitting in her familiar seat in the back row of the church that morning, knowing in her heart that this was her time. That evening she told her singles fellowship that their prayers were answered, and she was now trusting in Christ as her Lord and Savior.

Within a week as I was settling back into the routine of serving the church, I had a call from Kathy asking for an appointment, and I began to hear her story. Kathy and I had many conversations over the next two years. She grew spiritually and gave clear evidence by her life and witness that she was "born again." I still treasure a picture of her taken the day she joined the church, joyfully smiling, with her arms around Carl and me, who she called her "favorite men in the world." Following the service she gave a big party as an incentive to get all her old friends (including her former lover) to come to church. The disease took its toll, and eventually her body wasted away. In her final days she was lovingly cared for by members of her Sunday evening fellowship group. I served her Communion during the week, and that weekend, while I was away leading a seminar explaining spiritual birth, Kathy peacefully went home to heaven. It was my privilege to conduct Kathy's funeral and to tell her story to a large gathering that filled our church.

The simple analogy of comparing spiritual birth to physical birth is one I have been using in preaching, teaching, and personal conversation for over twenty years. It originally came together after a sermon I preached from John 3 (Jesus' conversation with Nicodemus), in which I tried to think through with the congregation what it means to actually *experience* the new birth Jesus talked about. In the congregation that morning were two members of the new ministry Prison Fellowship, which grew out of Charles Colson's highly publicized conversion (more about that later in the book). After the service they approached me and asked if I would give that same message to a group of inmates who would be coming to town. I still remember how they expressed their request. "There is no group of people who are more evangelized than those in prison. They are exhorted over and over to 'get saved' or 'give their hearts to Jesus.' But no one explains God's part in their getting saved. You just did, and we would like you to tell that to the inmates."

When I prepared to talk to the Prison Fellowship group, I illustrated my teaching by drawing a simple diagram that drew a parallel between physical and spiritual birth, which I believe was Jesus' intention in John 3. Little did I know it then, but that diagram (what I came to call the *birthline*) marked a turning point in the way I have done ministry ever since. It is not the diagram itself as much as the ideas it suggests that have had such an impact on my ministry.

My intention in writing this book is still the one I started with many years ago—to help understand in practical terms how people actually experience the new birth. We can study it biblically and theologically, but what does it look like in the lives of real people? This is the question that has faced me as a pastor and that those of you who are serving in prison ministries, youth work, as Bible study leaders, missionaries, and parents are dealing with every day. I have presented these ideas in many settings and have received insights and suggestions from people of all different backgrounds. What I am going to present in this book is the result of contributions from many, many people.

I believe the place to start in helping others is to try to understand as best we can just how the Spirit worked in *our* hearts. That is where I will begin. We will do some study of key Scripture passages, so that our experience is put into a biblical setting, and then I will ask you to reflect on how this has worked in your own experience.

For some of you, reading this may be your opportunity to consider whether or not *you* have been born again. Perhaps you have heard that phrase but are not quite sure what it means. Today people often make a distinction between Christians and "born again" Christians. What is the difference? Or is there a difference? I hope what I write will be helpful to you personally, even if you feel you are very much a beginner in the Christian walk.

The second part of the book will be an application to ministry. By *ministry* I don't necessarily mean the formal or ordained ministry. I mean those of you who are involved with people in a setting where you are discussing matters involving their spiritual standing before God. That applies to everyone who has experienced the new birth. God used others to bring you to faith, and you need to be available to be used in passing the faith along to yet others. In one chapter I want to speak particularly to parents and those involved with ministry to children from Christian homes about the spiritual birth of our children. The phrase I use to describe our involvement with the new birth of others is *spiritual midwives*. It is God who causes the birth, but we can be there to help the process along.

This book will be full of personal stories like the one I just told about Kathy. We all love to hear stories, and it could be tempting to skip the substance of the book and just read the stories. But every story I will relate is included to serve as a case study of the basic principles of the biblical teaching about the new birth. In particular I want to show how the Holy Spirit works *before* people actually exercise faith in Jesus, in what we usually call conversion. In the hundreds of settings where I have presented this idea it has seldom failed to be immediately recognized as true to people's personal experience. But what that actually looks like is as varied as the people themselves. As we will see, factors such as family, personal circumstances, and temperaments are all part of how the Spirit works. A variety of stories will make this truth clear, but they will also remind us that we should not expect particular experiences to be duplicated. I will offer an analysis of many of the stories, and I hope this will encourage you to begin thinking in the same way about your own story and those of people you are encountering in ministry or everyday life.

In the case of Kathy, for example, consider all the elements that led to her coming to faith in Christ. She was shocked into an awareness of her need for help (but not necessarily her need for a Savior), but she was able to express that to a Christian supervisor who was willing to share his faith. Kathy also experienced the reality of Christ's love and acceptance in a welcoming community even as she began to hear about it in preaching and teaching. And then, at just the right time, my story and the idea of the baby calling out gave her the nudge she needed to surrender her life to Christ and confess him to others. We can observe all of these pieces, but at the root of it all we also see the gracious working of God directing the whole process. Not many stories will be as dramatic as Kathy's, and not everyone has such a specific point of conversion as she did. But what will be common to all authentic experiences of the new birth is the inward work of the Holy Spirit bringing us to a simple but genuine faith in Jesus Christ as Lord and Savior.

In the end, we have to step back in amazement at the gracious work of God who finds us wandering and lost and brings us to himself. Reflect on the first three verses of John Newton's famous hymn, which is a testimony in song of his experience of the new birth. Notice in particular the words of the second verse, which is a recollection of God's grace *before* his conversion ("'Twas grace that taught my heart to fear, and grace my fears relieved"). But it is only *after* conversion ("the hour I first believed") that he began to appreciate that God had been seeking him before he was seeking God.

> Amazing grace!—how sweet the sound—
> That saved a wretch like me!
> I once was lost, but now am found,
> Was blind, but now I see.
>
> 'Twas grace that taught my heart to fear,
> And grace my fears relieved;
> How precious did that grace appear
> The hour I first believed.
>
> Thro' many dangers, toils, and snares,
> I have already come;
> 'Tis grace has brought me safe thus far,
> And grace will lead me home.
>
> —JOHN NEWTON, 1779

CHAPTER 2

The Birthline: A Sixty-five-Year Pregnancy

IN THE SUMMER OF 2000 my wife Sandy and I enjoyed attending the New Life Masih Ghar congregation in Southall, a community in the far western suburbs of London, now made up almost entirely of South Asians. Toward the end of our time at Masih Ghar, a distinguished gentleman with a white beard and turban marking him as a Punjabi Sikh started attending the services. I met him and only knew him as Mr. U. However, I followed his story with great interest, and during subsequent visits to London, I learned more of the details of his life and got to know two of his children.

After we left in 2000, Mr. U continued to attend Sunday services. After several months he spoke to Bob Heppe, the leader of the ministry, and requested baptism. Mr. U's profession of faith was a simple one—he trusted in Jesus for the forgiveness of his sin, and he desired to publicly confess that faith through baptism. The day of his baptism was a very special one, and he invited his children to attend, to their enormous surprise. The statement Mr. U prepared and had read on that day is included below.

After Mr. U's baptism, his children living in Southall began attending the church, and after a few months they too requested baptism. I learned from his daughter that Mr. U had been married, by arrangement, to a Roman Catholic woman who passed away before they came to England. Although they never spoke openly of religion in the home, she secretly taught the children the stories of Christmas and Easter. Clearly their hearts had been prepared to hear and receive the good news of Christ through this early influence of their mother and then the conversion of their father.

On a visit in 2005 I was invited to preach. Since I was working on this book, I presented a message from John 3 and explained the idea of the new birth, using the birthline as an illustration. I explained the idea of spiritual pregnancy, and as I mentioned the case of Mr. U. his son laughed out loud and said that *his father's pregnancy had lasted 65 years!* Here is his story in his own words.

THE TESTIMONY OF MR. U

My name is U__ Singh, and my aim of this testimony is the glory of Christ Jesus my Lord.

I was born into a Punjabi/Hindu family around the year 1914. As a child I had observed my mother doing religious duties to various Hindu deities, and I became a religiously minded person from such upbringing. During my early life I studied various religious scriptures from all the faiths: Hindus' holy book the Gita, Sikhs' holy book the Granth Sahab, Islamic holy book the Qur'an and Christians' holy book, the Holy Bible.

As any other person living in India, I was accustomed to the various traditions observed by the different faiths and taught rigorously by the various teachers, pier, fakirs, gianis and gurus.

All my working life and career has been in the British/Indian Army in the Sikh Light Infantry. So this job provided me with various opportunities to travel from India to Israel, mainly by ships and trucks/jeeps overland. It was during these "soldiers' years" that I received a gift of the Bible in Urdu from a Christ's servant in Lahore around the year 1935. I read it extensively and was particularly impressed by the life and teachings of Jesus Christ. I longed for a deep and real spiritual experience that would change my life. But this was not to happen till many years later.

It was in the year 2000 when I met several people from the New Life Masih Ghar in Southall Broadway when my search was again awakened. I obtained a booklet called *Consider Jesus* and started reading it a few days later. I was again reminded of the great words of Jesus Christ concerning life. One particular saying in this booklet that caught my mind and gripped my attention was subtitled: "He promises life after death: Jesus said, 'I am the life and the resurrection. He who believes in Me will live, even though he dies; and whoever lives and believes in Me will never die' (John 11:25–26)."

This promise from Jesus took hold of me strongly. It was absolutely unique. Who else is like him? I pondered over all my years (some eighty-six years now!) and all the places I had been, people I had met, and what they said of themselves and other great people and teachings—*but none had said anything like this!* I knew in my very heart this was what I had been seeking—a release from the repeated cycles of birth and death, which so often plagued me and tormented me. I knew Jesus' words of promise were strong and real, and truly *only* he could do this because he is the

Mukti Data (Savior of the world). I wanted him to be my savior (*Mukti Data*) too.

It was several months later (in November) that I confessed to the other followers of Christ that Jesus' promise as the Mukti Data is releasing me from the bondage and grip of this present world and giving me eternal life. I say, "At my age I have heard and seen many things, and now *the time has come for me to act upon it.* It is not time to start studying again, for the time is short to leave this world and enter another one—the presence and abode of God. So I believe with all my heart that Christ will fulfill his great promise of life to me and his hold on me will never loosen. I don't want to lose him either, or what he has done for me."

I hope this testimony will fill your heart with joy and cause you to consider Jesus in your life as your Savior and Lord.

As a small token of my love for Jesus, and what he has done for me, I take this symbol of baptism in obedience to his Word.

The Lord bless you all. *Permeshvar aap ko ashish de.*

THE BIRTH PROCESS

The stories of Kathy and Mr. U are dramatic examples of a process that takes place for everyone who is born again. To understand that process I have used a diagram that draws out the analogy of physical and spiritual birth. Take some time to examine the following diagram. As I mentioned in the last chapter, I first drew the birthline several years ago to help me explain the work of God in salvation to a group of prison inmates. Over the years I have refined and developed it, thanks to helpful suggestions from many people. But the simple concept of comparing physical and spiritual birth has stood the test of time and has proved invaluable in helping people understand the teaching of Jesus about the new birth. *Understanding this diagram is the key to understanding what I write in the rest of the book.*

Notice that I take the familiar process of physical birth—conception, pregnancy, delivery, and growth—as a means to understand the less familiar idea of spiritual birth. We will look in detail at Jesus' conversation with Nicodemus in the next chapter, but it seems obvious that when Jesus used the language of birth to describe the new life he came to bring, it was intended to provoke images of physical birth. That is certainly how Nicodemus reacted. I do not want to claim that the way I use the birthline to help understand our coming to faith is what Jesus was trying to teach in each detail, but this will help explain a pattern common to those who have experienced the new birth.

Take some time to examine the following diagram:

PHYSICAL AND SPIRITUAL BIRTH

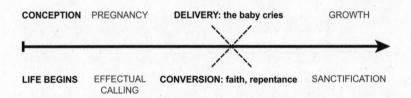

To benefit from what I will present in the rest of the book, you need to be familiar not only with the birthline illustration, but also with the definitions of the words I use. This is very important because in my studies I have discovered that different authors will use words like *regeneration* or *conversion*, but if I did not know what they meant in using them, I could misunderstand what they were teaching. I am not claiming that my use of the words is *the* correct use; I am only saying that you need to make sure you understand the way I use these familiar concepts in order to understand the teaching represented in the birthline.

This is a discussion of what theologians call the *application of redemption*. That means it is a description of how God the Holy Spirit applies the redemption that God the Father planned that was made possible through the coming to earth of God the Son. This is salvation by God's amazing grace—his undeserved favor. That grace is all the more amazing when we realize that our salvation is a work of all three persons of the Holy Trinity.[1] If this was a book about the totality of God's saving work, we would need to study the love of God the Father, who "chose us in him before the creation of the world," and the sacrifice of God the Son, in whom "we have redemption through his blood" (Eph. 1:3–10). But in this book I am concentrating attention on the specific ministry of God the Holy Spirit to those who have not yet come to the point of conversion.

The first thing to note from the birthline is the obvious fact that spiritual birth, just like physical birth, is fundamentally a *process*. The delivery of the baby is an important *event*, but it is clearly understood to be the result of something that took place earlier followed by a season of gestation (pregnancy). Furthermore, the event of the delivery is not the end of the process

1. I explain this in a booklet, *What Is True Conversion?* (Phillipsburg, NJ: P&R Publishing), 2005. I make the point that experientially we encounter God in the reverse order that we usually discuss him. Our first encounter with God is the Holy Spirit (even though we don't know it at the time), who leads us to the Son; and through the Son we come to know God as Father.

but is just the beginning of a new chapter in a life begun nine months earlier. In evangelical Christianity, which is the heritage of many of us, there has been such an emphasis on conversion as an event, with particular attention given to dramatic conversions, that thinking of spiritual birth as a process is a very important paradigm shift. Stop and reflect on how much that is written about the Christian life is rooted in language such as, "*when* you accepted Christ as your Savior . . ." or "the *moment* you gave your heart to Christ . . ."

Almost without exception when I present this basic idea of coming to Christ as a process, there is instant acknowledgment from my listeners. I watch heads nod in agreement as people begin to recall the ways God worked in their hearts prior to their actual conversion. The reason this seems to come as such a revelation is that almost all the teaching many have received marks the beginning of the spiritual life as conversion. Or there is an assumption that the new birth and conversion are the same thing, which is not the case. So there is a disconnect between what people have been taught and what they have actually experienced. This also applies to the way much evangelism is taught. People are told that their goal is to briefly present biblical truth and then press others to pray a prayer, with little account made of the need for hearts to be prepared by the Holy Spirit. Again, this is teaching that does not fit with people's personal experience, nor does it seem to work when they try to evangelize others. We will discuss all of this in greater detail, but at this stage simply recognize the importance of beginning to think in terms of *process* rather than *event*.

As the diagram notes, the term I am using for God's inner work is *regeneration*. I will not try to be more precise than that. Theologians have argued over the centuries about just when to fix the moment of regeneration, or whether it is the beginning of salvation or the whole process. Ultimately regeneration is an invisible and supernatural work of God. Therefore, without trying to be too technical, regeneration is what my friends from Prison Fellowship described as "God's part of salvation."

The key to the entire birth process is *conception* (note the diagram). That is when life begins. Physically this is a private matter, and it is only known that there is a new life growing some time after it has actually happened. Spiritually the beginning of a new life is even more mysterious. Jesus used the imagery of the blowing of the wind to describe it. At this point we step onto holy ground because God Almighty, the Lord of all creation, actually comes to a human being and breathes spiritual life into the soul. At first this new life is totally hidden away, and it is only over time that we begin to sense that something is different.

The process of coming to a conscious faith, once the work of God has begun, is what could be thought of as spiritual pregnancy. The term I use for this season of our spiritual life is *calling*. In the older language of the Westminster Confession of Faith, the term for this is *effectual* calling, which simply means *it works*: when God calls, *we come*. We will discuss calling in some detail, but it includes conviction of sin, understanding the gospel, and a changing of our desires so that we want Christ. Unlike a physical pregnancy, the length of which is fairly fixed, spiritual pregnancy goes on as briefly or as long as it takes God to bring us to faith and repentance. He uses the prayers of others, the witness of friends and family, the preaching of the Word, and even suffering to bring us to this place. But once we finally come to a vital faith, we can look back and see God's hand at work long before we believed.

Physically, we know that what is conceived grows for about nine months. A crossing then occurs (indicated by the dotted X on the birthline diagram) from one phase of life to another phase of life. The baby has been alive for some time, but now it is time to go public. We often speak of that as the *birth* of the baby, but we recognize that this is really the end of the first phase of the whole growth process. It is essentially the same pattern with the life of a Christian. Once God has begun the process, there is a time of preparation, essentially a *spiritual pregnancy*, and finally a visible expression of that new life as we turn to Christ in faith and turn away from a life of unbelief and disobedience. This experience of turning is what is usually thought of as *conversion*. We will discuss the various ways people experience conversion. The reason I draw the X as a dotted line is that the more conversion stories I heard, the more I realized that many, if not most, people cannot specifically identify a point at which they were converted even though they know a change has taken place. It is very important to have a conscious sense of having trusted Christ, but since conversion, or the act of trusting Christ, is a *result* of the inner work of the Spirit, the actual experience of conversion is not the critical issue. It is the cry of the newborn baby that follows months of pregnancy.

Finally, the birthline diagram makes the obvious point that one who is alive grows up. Growth is a slow process, with many starts and stops, but the day of delivery is the beginning of a new phase in the overall process. The discussion of Christian growth (*sanctification*) is not the primary purpose of this book, but it must be noted that the birthline diagram makes an assumption, consistent with Scripture, that those who come to faith in Christ are on a path that inevitably leads to the growth of that faith.

Readers with theological training can see that this presentation of regeneration raises many issues that could lead to a great
deal more discussion. However, my purpose is to offer more
of a handbook that will be helpful to those wrestling with the
question of their own spiritual birth as well as how to be helpful
to others. Every major Christian tradition I have studied agrees
that salvation comes to us through the gracious initiative of God.
Each tradition has some way of describing the work of God in
the soul before we are actually converted.

Here is a wonderful hymn that I first became acquainted
with in a Presbyterian hymnal, but then found in hymnals of
the Mennonite church and the Free Methodists. It represents
the heart cry of all those who have been born again by the Spirit,
whatever their particular tradition may be.

> I sought the Lord, and afterward I knew
> He moved my soul to seek him, seeking me;
> It was not I that found, O Savior true;
> No, I was found of thee.
>
> Thou didst reach forth thy hand and mine enfold;
> I walked and sank not on the storm-vexed sea—
> 'Twas not so much that I on thee took hold,
> As thou, dear Lord, on me.
>
> I find, I walk, I love, but O the whole of love
> Is but my answer, Lord, to thee;
> For thou wert long beforehand with my soul,
> Always thou lovedst me.

—ANONYMOUS, 1878

PART ONE

HOW THE SPIRIT WORKS IN CONVERSION

CHAPTER 3

A Study in Scripture: Jesus' Meeting with Nicodemus

ONE OF THE MOST MOVING conversion stories I have come across I encountered in reading *The Autobiography of Malcolm X*. *The Autobiography* is the story of Malcolm Little, a man who changed the trajectory of the civil rights struggle in the 1950s. Shortly after he was killed in 1965 by other Black Muslims, his story appeared and became standard reading for a generation (it was also a movie directed by Spike Lee). Malcolm's conversion took place while he was in prison. He wrote about his deep conviction of sin until he finally bowed the knee to ask forgiveness of God. "You know what my life had been. Picking a lock to rob someone's house was the only way my knees had ever been bent before. I had to force myself to bend my knees. And waves of shame and embarrassment would force me back up. For evil to bend its knees, admitting its guilt, to implore the forgiveness of God, is the hardest thing in the world." But he finally submitted, and at that point his life took on a whole new purpose. He wrote, "I still marvel at how swiftly my previous life's thinking pattern slid away from me, like snow sliding off a roof. . . . I would be startled to catch myself thinking in a remote way of my earlier self as another person."[1] The chapter in which he describes his conversion is entitled, "Saved." But while it is a wonderful conversion testimony, *it was conversion to Islam*, not to Christ. Malcolm X went on to become the leader of the Nation of Islam or Black Muslims.

Reading that conversion account shocked me because I had always assumed that such experiences were reserved for Christian conversions. But religious encounters, including conversion experiences, are something that is part of our humanity. In our own day we are living in a time of great interest in "spirituality" and spiritual experiences. We must have some means of discerning what is genuine spirituality, rooted in the work of the Holy Spirit and leading to faith in Christ, and what is a false or merely human spirituality. *We have this means in the Scriptures.* The Bible is our divinely given "textbook" for understanding how God works in the souls of those he calls to himself.

It is important that we stop and study our textbook before we go further in the discussion of experience. It must be the Scriptures that inform and interpret our experience rather than our experience that shapes our reading of Scripture. The assumption that the Bible is divinely inspired and authoritative was fundamental to the teaching of Jesus as well as to the apostle Paul. Through the years this has been the church's objective foundation for all teaching, and I stand in the same place. Before

1. Alex Haley, *The Autobiography of Malcolm X* (New York: Ballantine Books, 1973), 169–70.

we become students of human spiritual experience, we need to be students of the Bible.

> All Scripture is God-breathed and is useful for teaching, rebuking, correcting and training in righteousness, so that the man of God may be thoroughly equipped for every good work. (2 Tim. 3:16–17)

In this chapter I invite you to consider carefully Jesus' meeting with Nicodemus, recorded in John 3. This passage is the basis for the idea of the spiritual birthline. In the second part of the book, when we consider how to be spiritual midwives, we will look at some passages from Paul as he describes his ministry. I believe there is greater value in concentrating on a few passages than quickly looking at a large number of proof texts. Undoubtedly many other portions of Scripture can and should be studied, and I will suggest some of them. Whether you are reading this as an individual or as a group, the next step in learning about the new birth is to open your Bible and devote some serious attention to what God has revealed through his Word.

Keep in mind that for the most part these are passages describing what *needs to be experienced* (as in the case of Nicodemus) or what *has already been experienced* (as in the letters of Paul to new believers). The issue therefore, is not the objective truth of Scripture *or* our experience. It is learning to understand the truth of Scripture in order to understand our experience and that of others. However, even as we study Scripture, we need to acknowledge that while we seek to be objective, our reading of Scripture will be influenced by our circumstances and traditions. But at least we need to do our best to begin from a biblical perspective. Older writers spoke of the pastor as "the physician of the soul." The idea behind that phrase is that a skilled pastor knew God's Word, but he was also skilled in understanding how its truth applied to different people and situations. Whether or not we are pastors, we need to know the teaching of Scripture and do our best to apply it properly.

JOHN 3:1–8

[1]Now there was a man of the Pharisees named Nicodemus, a member of the Jewish ruling council. [2]He came to Jesus at night and said, "Rabbi, we know you are a teacher who has come from God. For no one could perform the miraculous signs you are doing if God were not with him."

[3]In reply Jesus declared, "I tell you the truth, no one can see the kingdom of God unless he is born again."

[4]"How can a man be born when he is old?" Nicodemus asked. "Surely he cannot enter a second time into his mother's womb to be born!"

[5]Jesus answered, "I tell you the truth, no one can enter the kingdom of God unless he is born of water and the Spirit. [6]Flesh gives birth to flesh, but the Spirit gives birth to spirit. [7]You should not be surprised at my saying, 'You must be born again.' [8]The wind blows wherever it pleases. You hear its sound, but you cannot tell where it comes from or where it is going. So it is with everyone born of the Spirit."

Introduction

This is the most important passage for our study, and I encourage you to take the time to understand it thoroughly. It is the teaching from Jesus himself, from which all the discussion of "born-again Christians" comes, and it is also the basis for the birthline diagram.

The concept of the new birth is basic to John's writings and has already been mentioned in the introduction to his Gospel (1:12–13) and is the core of his letters (1, 2, 3 John). The passage in John 3 comes to us as a conversation between Jesus and a prominent Jewish religious leader, a Pharisee named Nicodemus. The text says Nicodemus came to Jesus at night. This was either to avoid the stigma of being seen with Jesus or, more likely, so he would have an opportunity for an extended conversation.

Keep in mind that the setting of this conversation is during the ministry of John the Baptist, who announced the coming kingdom of God and insisted on baptism as a sign of repentance in order to prepare for it. Any mention of the kingdom got the attention of Jewish people because this was the long-awaited fulfillment of God's promise to come to earth and restore his *shalom*, or peace, to a broken and chaotic world. For reasons we are not told, Nicodemus felt drawn to Jesus rather than rejecting him as so many of his fellow Pharisees were doing. He believed Jesus had something to teach him about the kingdom, but what he heard was not what he expected.

When told he must be "born again" in order to see the kingdom of God, Nicodemus immediately thought of physical birth (v. 4). This was obviously what Jesus intended. As the master teacher, he started with the known, then moved to the unknown. So it is true to Jesus' intention to use physical birth to understand spiritual birth.

Study of the Passage

Stop and read slowly through the passage at least twice.

Give careful attention to the explanation Jesus gave in verses 5–8:

verse 5. Jesus repeated the words "I tell you the truth" ("Truly, truly" in other translations) for emphasis and again mentioned entering or seeing the kingdom of God (there is probably no difference between the two ideas). But Jesus wanted to make it clear that this was a matter of the utmost importance.

We need to give particular attention to the Greek words used for "born" (used eight times in this passage; vv. 3, 4 [twice], 5, 6 [twice], 7, 8) and "again" (vv. 3, 7). The word translated "born" is from the Greek verb *gennao*, which means "to generate" or to give life to a new generation (thus the term *regeneration*). It is used in the older language of "Abraham *begat* Isaac; and Isaac *begat* Jacob" (see Matt. 1:2–16 KJV). The idea is closer to that of the conception of a child than actually giving birth, although both ideas are included. In this passage every time the verb appears, it is in the *passive* voice. That means we are not the ones who do the begetting or birthing—it is what happens to us because of the action of another.

The second word, "again," is the Greek word *anothen*, which can be also translated "from above." Putting together these two key words can have several possible translations: "born again," "born from above," "begotten again," or "begotten from above." The last possibility may be the most precise translation. In any case Jesus was not describing what *we* must do but what must happen *to us*. This is very consistent with the other words in the passage.

In verse 5 the word "Spirit" is capitalized in most translations, even though there is no capitalization in the Greek text, because it is clearly a reference to the Holy Spirit as the one who causes the birth. The new birth, therefore, is not an inward reformation or a reference to reincarnation but is an activity of the Holy Spirit. In some respects the miraculous virgin birth of Jesus when he was "conceived . . . from the Holy Spirit" (Matt. 1:20) was a picture of this work of the Spirit. Spiritual life is supernaturally begun in us "from above."

"Born of water" has several possible interpretations. It could be physical birth (the child carried in the water sac), although that is not likely. Another possibility is that Jesus is referring to a well-known prophecy of the kingdom in Ezekiel 36 in which the Lord says that in that day he would not only "sprinkle clean water on you" but would also "give you a new heart" and "put a new spirit in you; I will remove from you your heart of stone and give you a heart of flesh. And I will put my Spirit in you" (vv. 25–27). Perhaps this is why Jesus chided Nicodemus for not understanding what he was saying (John 3:9–10), since a teacher of Israel would certainly know this promise.

It is my view that Jesus is referring to baptism, but specifically to the baptism of John, which was a baptism for repentance. It was an act required of those converting to Judaism at that time. John was saying that in the light of the coming kingdom, Jews needed to repent and be converted to their own religion. Jesus agreed with John about the need for repentance but was adding that something *more* was needed—a birth by the Spirit—as prophesied by Ezekiel.

Throughout much of church history, many have understood this verse to refer to Christian baptism. This is a key text for those who make baptism the starting point of regeneration; hence the phrase *baptismal regeneration*. In this view the water of baptism is not only a sign of the Spirit's coming but actually causes the Spirit to come, so that birth by water *is* birth by the Spirit. I will talk about the importance of baptism, but I agree with those who do not think that Christian baptism is in view in this text.

But whatever the meaning (and this could even be true for those who insist it means Christian baptism), the main issue is that birth by water is not sufficient. There must be a second birth, a birth from above—that which is of "the Spirit."

verse 6. To emphasize the point, Jesus makes a clear distinction between the human ("flesh") experience of birth and birth by the Spirit (literally, "that which *has been begotten* by the flesh . . . that which *has been begotten* by the Spirit"). Note again how most translations use capitalization to make the point: "That which is born of the Spirit is spirit." Human life comes through the flesh, and spiritual life comes through the Spirit.

verse 7. A careful look at this verse is significant in the practical application of the meaning of spiritual birth. Thus far it is clear that the new birth is totally a work of the Holy Spirit. Like our physical birth, we are present, but there is nothing we do to cause it. But a superficial reading of verse 7 seems to suggest that Jesus is now telling Nicodemus that he needed to make this happen. ("I am saying to you—be born again!") But this verse is *not* a command. Grammatically, verse 7 is in the indicative mode, making a statement, not the imperative mood, which gives a command. The second "you" of the verse is plural. So a literal reading of verse 7 is, "Nicodemus, don't be surprised that I am telling you [singular] that it is necessary for you [plural] to be born again." This is a statement of what must happen to anyone in order to enter the kingdom of God. But Jesus has already made it clear that such a birth comes only through the Spirit. Therefore, the new birth is something the Spirit does *for* people; it is not something people do for themselves. It is not an act of cooperation. God acts in the human soul where there was no life and begets life.

44

verse 8. This is one of the most sublime verses of all Scripture, and it reinforces the truth that the new birth is a supernatural work. It is a deliberate play on words because "wind" and "Spirit" is the same word in the Greek (*pneuma*). Just as we do not know where the wind comes from and only see its effects, so we must recognize that ultimately the new birth is a mystery of God at work in the human soul. We will see the effects of that work because such a person will believe in Jesus, as the passage itself goes on to explain (3:14–18), along with other manifestations of new life (the theme of 1 John). But the new birth itself, *regeneration*, is God's work alone. As pastor John Piper explains, "his begetting causes our believing."[2]

Implications of the Passage

I have labored to point out the supernatural character of the new birth because it is a very common error to confuse the new birth (regeneration) and the human response of faith in Christ (conversion). This is not simply a matter of theological precision. *As a practical issue we need to be reminded that we cannot make people become Christians.* We cannot describe steps people should take so they can be born again. Much harm has been done, even when well intended, by those determined to press on unwilling or unprepared people the need to pray a prayer or say particular words so they will become "born-again Christians." The importance of faith and repentance in conversion will be discussed, but for now recognize that John 3:1–8 is *not* about the human role in salvation.

If you are struggling with the question of whether or not you have been born again, this passage should give you hope. One

2. John Piper, *Finally Alive* (Fearn, Tain, Ross-Shire, Christian Focus, 2009), 105. Dr. Piper's book is a theologically precise but pastorally oriented study of the new birth.

mark of the Spirit's working is that we move from an expectation that we need to make ourselves worthy of God's salvation to recognizing that we are helpless to change ourselves. But the work of the Spirit changes us from within—the very thing we cannot do. So if you are sensing that you are being drawn toward Christ but know you cannot get there by yourself, feel encouraged. God is more powerful than even your sin and rebellion.

I have also found that awareness of the truth of this passage has been both reassuring and encouraging to those seriously engaged in the work of pointing others to Christ. On the one hand it is reassuring to know that ultimately this is a work of God and is not dependent on our words or skills. We feel very inadequate when engaging with people's spiritual destiny, and the fact of the matter is, *we are inadequate!* (But see 2 Cor. 2:16; 3:4–6.) But we are also encouraged because in a way that is as mysterious as the blowing of the wind, God uses inadequate people as part of the accomplishment of his great work of causing the kingdom to come, one life at a time. Just like a midwife helping in the delivery of a baby, we are available to participate in God's work and to be in awe of his power to give new life to those "dead in . . . transgressions and sins" (Eph. 2:1, 4–5).

When we understand the new birth as Jesus presents it, we should realize that we are in the realm of miracle in the purest sense of that word. As someone once remarked to me after a discussion of the implications of the birthline, "This is holy ground—God has come and is in our midst." Consideration of the new birth should cause us to worship the God who has been pleased to come to us. Not only has he come near by giving his dearly beloved Son, but also he has come near, and is coming near, in the person of the Holy Spirit. In addition to worship, we should have a new appreciation of the importance of prayers of intercession. Part of the mystery of God's work is that his purposes are accomplished as his people pray. Therefore we need to come with renewed faith to pray for his saving power to be at work. This is praying "Your kingdom come" at the most essential level.

Keep in view the initial statement of Jesus that the new birth is how we enter *the kingdom of God*. The kingdom, where Jesus rules on earth even as he rules in heaven, is the greater issue. The new birth is the doorway, and it is terribly important that we enter through the right door. But our new birth is part of a greater work that God is doing. That means we begin with a personal work of God in the individual, but it should not end with the individual. I will have more to say about this important truth later (chapter 14).

AN APPLICATION

The most common way I introduce the birthline is by starting with a brief Bible study in John 3. In American popular culture, as well as in many other places, the phrase *born again* is known even though people usually have no idea what it means. Even in a churched culture, it is used without much real understanding. I begin my presentation with references to uses of "born again" in the culture or simply comment that this is a phrase we use even though we don't understand it. Then I take them to John 3:1–8 for Jesus' definition of the term. I don't go into all the detail I have just given, but I work through the verses in such a way that people see clearly that being born again is not something we do but what the Spirit does in us. This is obvious from the passage, but typically it comes as a new insight to most of the group because we tend to be so focused on what we can do for God.

Early in the presentation I point out that when Nicodemus was first confronted by the phrase "born again," he thought immediately of physical birth. But then I explain verses 5–7 and wait until after we have discussed verse 8 to go back to that idea and present the birthline. I point out that in verse 8 Jesus says that we can't actually see the Spirit, just as we can't see the wind; but we can see the *effects* of the wind. In the same way, even though we can't see the actual change brought by the Spirit, we can understand something of what it looks like by thinking about physical birth. I then pass out a copy of the birthline diagram, describing the process of physical birth and how it applies to spiritual birth.

For years I have done this as the first lesson in a new members class at the churches I have served as pastor. I end by asking people if the birthline has helped them understand their own spiritual pilgrimage and if they can actually put themselves somewhere on the line. That may create some discussion at the time, but it also gives me a starting point for conversations with people for the remainder of the classes. I will simply ask if the birthline was helpful (which it is for most) or confusing, but that question always allows a discussion of where people see themselves in the process of the new birth. As I noted above, the idea of coming to Christ as a process more than an event has proven very helpful to people, including people who are not yet ready to commit to Christ but have a sense that God is working in their hearts. Keep in mind that how people view themselves may not be the same as where they actually are or (most importantly) how God sees them. Nevertheless, the birthline is a tool for reflecting on our relationship with God, and many have found it helpful.

CHAPTER 4

Knowing and Telling
Our Own Story

I WAS INVITED TO DINNER one evening to reestablish contact with members of my extended family whom I hadn't seen in years. We enjoyed good conversation as we caught up on news of our children and grandchildren and our life activities. At one point one of my relatives asked what had caused me to go into the ministry. I hadn't gone to the dinner with the intention of preaching to my family, but I took the opportunity afforded by the question to tell my story.

I told them about my nonreligious background, trying to invite comments about how religion and church had been experienced in their families. I described my first introduction to committed Christians and many of the personal struggles and questions that eventually led to my believing in Christ. I told about my conversion experience, but in a way that suggested there were other ways to hear and believe the gospel. Finally I answered the question that was initially asked, and I described my going into the ministry. In the end, I not only told my story but was able to do it in such a way that allowed almost everyone else in the group to talk about where they were spiritually. We had a very lively conversation, and we all went away with some things to think about.

I relate this incident because it introduces the value of knowing our own stories well enough to retell them in any number of settings. However, the primary value of knowing the story of our rebirth is for our own appreciation of the depth of God's love for us, revealed in a way that was particularly suited to speak to our hearts. God not only loved the world so much that he sent his only Son, but he loved us so much that he "sent the Spirit of his Son into our hearts" to give us new life and then bring us to the place where we cry out, "Abba, Father" (Gal. 4:4–7). This deepening understanding will lead us to speak praise to God, but it will also help us tell our story to others in a natural and winsome way.

KNOWING YOUR STORY

When I teach the birthline in seminar or classroom settings, I try to take a significant amount of time after the presentation to allow members of the group to tell what the process of spiritual birth has looked like in their own lives. Almost inevitably this causes people to look farther and farther back into their lives to recall ways the Spirit was at work preparing them. Many times people have only thought about the things immediately surrounding their actual conversion, and the insights gained from the birthline give them a whole new appreciation of the extent of God's reaching out to them.

I remember one seminar where a man came to me to tell me that our discussion had given him freedom to be genuinely thankful for his family for the first time. He described a very zealous and closed fundamentalist family that had strict rules for everything. They would not tolerate any nonconformity, and in the end Bill said he felt forced out and left home as an angry young man. Bill went down many paths that he was not proud of and finally came to genuine faith as an adult. "But now I realize," he said, "that it was with my family that I first heard the gospel, and try as hard as I could, I was never able to escape those truths. Imperfect as my family members were, they were God's instruments to plant the first seeds of my spiritual life."

Not only does the teaching based on the birthline give new insight into the elements of God's calling, it has also allowed people to take a new look at their conversion. I'm one of those who can recall praying "the sinner's prayer" and receiving an immediate sense of relief. This is the classic form that conversion is supposed to take and, as I mentioned in my explanation of the birthline, I originally identified conversion as a solid X that crossed the line. However, as I have asked people to tell me about their actual point of conversion, it has been surprising to learn how few have actually "prayed the prayer" for conversion, even though they knew they were in a different place than before. Some have prayed the prayer so many times, they are confused as to which time it really "took," while others have nothing that could be described as a conversion experience and yet are committed followers of Christ.

Try to think of how to describe that place in your pilgrimage when you passed over from unbelief to belief or when truths you believed all your life became personal and affected how you lived. Then think about how you moved from conversion into growth as a believer. When we are born again, as defined by the Bible, it is inevitable that we will grow. Walking a new path is not optional when we are alive in Christ—it *will* happen. But what that actually looks like is different for all of us. Many look back on what they consider to be a genuine conversion early in life, but then they went through a time when that life was virtually dormant until many years later. In some cases that involves seriously straying from the path that could be identified as Christian, all the while knowing that they would *have* to come back at some point. Others will remember some sort of decision but don't think of that as the point of conversion. Often the most significant experiences of spiritual encounter come well after the time of conversion and even cause people to wonder which experience was their real conversion. Does it really matter? I don't think it does. In suggesting all of these possibilities I am trying to help us think about God's grace in our lives before, during, and after conversion rather than dwelling on one defining experience.

One effect of formulating our stories after considering the birthline is that it puts the focus on the work of God rather than on steps or decisions we have made. This is as it should be. Too often in testimonies we find ourselves talking essentially about ourselves and how we found God. The real story is how God came to find us. This should also serve to remind us of the amazing patience and perseverance of God in accomplishing his purpose for us, something that is very important to appreciate when we begin to consider how to help others come to Christ.

TELLING YOUR STORY

For a number of years I led a program in the church where I was pastor that we called Living for the King. Since the first step to living for the King is *entering* the kingdom, we began the course with a study of the new birth. I asked the members of the class to think through their own stories in relationship to the birthline, which they then talked about in their small groups. The next assignment was to prayerfully consider someone else to tell their story to—perhaps a family member or someone at work; it could be a fellow believer or an unbeliever. They could even begin the conversation by asking the person if they would help them complete an assignment for a class they were taking.

One year, in the session that followed that assignment, Dave, one of the members of the class, excitedly told of his experience that week. He decided to call his mother, with whom he had become alienated since his conversion. Dave had grown up in a nominal Roman Catholic family but had come to personal faith as an adult in a dramatic conversion experience. Wanting to see others have that same experience, he became involved in a zealous Protestant ministry that had supported him in doing whatever it took to win his family to Christ. Dave was sincere, but the end result was that he was forbidden to talk about religion whenever he gathered with the family.

However, in this phone conversation Dave told his mother that he was trying to understand his spiritual heritage and asked her to tell him more about his family background. This was a very sincere question from Dave because thinking through the birthline caused him to realize that the manner of his conversion had made him discount any spiritual influence from his home. So Dave listened and asked more questions and soon was hearing about his mother's spiritual journey. Then she asked Dave to tell her more about what he had come to believe, and he told his story as simply as he could and in a way that would make sense to his mother.

Dave reported to the group that the conversation ended up being two hours long and seemed to melt the walls of alienation. As the conversation ended, his mother mentioned how good it had been to talk to him and then said, "Dave, we thought we had lost you."

In response to a recent communication with Dave, asking permission to include this incident, he wrote, "For me, the birthline model's value was that it provided an effective framework and conversational approach for talking about issues of faith with my mom that engaged her rather than pushed her away. Looking back, I believe it is possible that God allowed our conversation to reverberate in her mind for the last eighteen months of her life and we saw the evidence of some fruits right near the very end of her days."

People talk constantly about their family and influences of childhood, about church and religion, and about what they are going through at the moment. We need to have thought about how God has worked in our lives so that we talk about this in a natural way. After all, this is simply our life. There are times when that will cause people to want to ask more substantial questions, as in my conversation with my relatives or Dave's with his mother. Often it will be just passed over as information. But the challenge is to be ready to tell our story or parts of it in ordinary conversation as well as on those occasions when we are able to give the long version.

Consider the example of the apostle Paul. The actual event of his conversion is told in Acts 9. Later in Acts there is a record of two different times when Paul tells his story to others (Acts 22, 26), and there can be little doubt that he did this on many other occasions. His letters are full of references to his background and how God had worked in his life and was working at the time he wrote. Paul knew how to tell his story in a way that made people think about their own relationship to God.

The only problem with calling attention to Paul, or anyone with a more dramatic conversion, is that people whose conversion is not so dramatic feel intimidated. *But everyone who is born again has a wonderful story to tell.* This is true because the heart of our story is God's grace at work through the Spirit, not of particular experiences. There is great value in hearing people's stories, but whenever I arrange for these stories, I'm always careful to include at least one person from a godly Christian home who cannot describe a point of conversion. Usually those people are reluctant because they insist their testimony is "boring." Thank God for "boring" testimonies!

GIRL MEETS GOD

A wonderful example of a person who both understands her story and knows how to tell it is Lauren F. Winner.[1] Raised with a nominal Jewish background, she later converted to Orthodox Judaism as a college student. But even before that conversion, she began to feel the compelling call to follow Jesus. This is all told beautifully in a memoir she wrote in 2002, *Girl Meets God.* In the endorsements at the beginning of the book, it is striking to read how many secular reviewers were drawn to her story even though the centrality of Jesus is very clear.

I enjoyed the telling of her story, but I particularly appreciated how thoughtfully she tried to interpret what God was doing in her life. At one point she comments that her boyfriend, an

---

1. Dr. Winner is currently Assistant Professor of Christian Spirituality at Duke Divinity School.

Orthodox Jew, seemed to have a better perspective of what was happening to her than she did. "At the time, I thought Dov was overreacting. Now I think he could see something I could not see. He could see Jesus slowly goading me toward Him."[2]

> Evangelical friends of mine are always trying to trim the corners and smooth the rough edges of what they call My Witness in order to shove it into a tidy, born-again conversion narrative. . . . I had no epiphanic on-the-road-to-Damascus experience. I can't tell my friends that I became a Christian January 8, 1993, or on my twentieth birthday. What I can tell them is that I grew up Jewish. I can tell them about the time I dreamed of Jesus rescuing me from a kidnapping. . . . I can tell them about reading *At Home in Mitford*, a charming if somewhat saccharine novel about an Episcopal priest in North Carolina, a novel that left me wanting something Christians seemed to have. I can tell them about my baptism.[3]

The reference to the well-known Mitford novels is significant. It is quite apparent in reading *Girl Meets God* that Winner thought of herself as a very intellectual and literate person. So the Lord used literature as one of the means to penetrate her shell. But rather than classic literature, he used what she calls "a charming if somewhat saccharine novel." She *happened* to pick it up in a display case as she was in a bookstore, read the first chapter, and then purchased two books in the series. She

> spent the next week reading and rereading the Mitford books. They were . . . vignettes about the people in Father Tim's parish, stories about ordinary Christians working out ordinary faith in

2. Lauren F. Winner, *Girl Meets God* (New York: Random House, 2003), 55.
3. Ibid., 7–8.

their ordinary lives. . . . They sang hymns I didn't know, and prayed from a prayer book I had never opened. And I thought, *I want what they have.*[4]

This is a wonderful example of how God graciously breaks into our lives in a manner that brings the gospel before us in unexpected ways. And Winner does a wonderful job of weaving them into her story. "He was laying traps, leaving clues, clues I could have seen had I been perceptive enough. . . . Sometimes, as in a great novel, you cannot see until you get to the end that God was leaving clues for you all along."[5]

AN APPLICATION

I encourage you to take some time to write your spiritual autobiography. You may want to finish this book first, or it could be a project you start doing now. Give yourself the opportunity to do some careful reflection about the work of God in your life. For most of us, writing is a way to let that happen. Begin with your family, which may make you think about earlier generations and the religious or spiritual influences that were already present (or absent) before you were born. What were the earliest impressions from your home? What were your own thoughts as you grew up? What about early impressions from church or other religious institutions? Trace all of these paths in your life

4. Ibid., 60.
5. Ibid., 57. Another thoughtfully written conversion story of an articulate, highly intelligent woman is *The Secret Thoughts of an Unlikely Convert* by Rosaria Champagne Butterfield (Crown and Covenant Publications, 2012). Mrs. Butterfield went from being a radical lesbian college professor to the wife of a Presbyterian pastor, and tells the story in a very compelling way.

up to the present. Think again about the time of your conversion. If you didn't have a specific conversion experience, why do you consider yourself converted? And if you did have a time of conversion, how do you know it was authentic? Recall some of the first steps, struggles, and doubts as you began a Christian walk. As you write, don't feel a need to fit your life into a preconceived pattern, including the birthline. Just tell your story as you recall it.

This first edition of your autobiography is just for your benefit. Write in a way that makes sense to you and in language that is straightforward and not full of religious jargon. This will be an unfinished story, especially if you are still wondering if you are born again, but write about what you understand at this stage of your spiritual growth. And realize that this is not necessarily how God sees you—it is merely your interpretation of what God seems to be doing.

CHAPTER 5

The Role of the Christian Community

BILL FRAZER FOUND himself at age thirty-one with every-thing a man could ask for. He was making an excellent salary, he was appointed to a very influential government position for someone his age, and he had a number of women friends with whom he was intimate. But if this was the pinnacle of life, something was missing. Where was the joy and satisfaction that he thought such a lifestyle should bring?

Around this time, he remembered a trip he'd taken two years earlier to visit an old college roommate who lived in Dallas, Texas. This trip came to mind because during that trip he met people who seemed to have the inner joy that was missing in his own life. His original expectations for that trip were to party with his old buddy in Dallas. Instead, his friend invited him to join a group of his friends who were spending the day fixing up a daycare center in inner-city Dallas. The next day he went with them to church (only after being promised a brunch afterward). To his great surprise, not only did he find this weekend trip fulfilling, but he also sensed that this group had the "something" he was missing—they reflected a genuine inner joy.

Could he find people like that in Washington, DC? Could he get the inner joy they had? The problem was, he didn't know what it was or where to get it. Since those people in Dallas were connected with a church, he began visiting churches to find what he was looking for, but without finding it. Finally his housemate found out about Bill's search and invited him to join him and his girlfriend to go to church (followed by brunch—a key element of Bill's pilgrimage, as he tells it). That happened to be the church I was pastoring at the time, and Bill told me that he still remembers two things about the first visit. First, he was asked to open a Bible and follow a text during the sermon, which he found far more interesting than he had expected. Second, as the people spoke to him and one another, he felt that same undefined joy that had caught his attention in Dallas. These people had the "something" he was looking for.

He continued attending for several months, learning more and more and enjoying the fellowship of his visits. It finally occurred to him that it would be a good idea to actually join the church, and he enrolled in the New Members Class. It was during this class that Bill finally understood the implications of Christ's death on the cross. The light went on one day as he was doing the assigned reading for that class. He read about the unblemished lambs that the Jews were to sacrifice for their sins and how Jesus was the Lamb of God sacrificed for our sins. Bill made a confession of his faith to the elders of the church as a public expression of a personal faith that had become his.

It has been my privilege to watch Bill grow in faith over several years and to see that develop into a zeal for reaching out to friends and others. He eventually took a number of trips to Russia, lived there for several years, and participated in the formation and growth of several churches. He is currently active in his local church and teaches a group of seekers who are coming to church for the same reason he did.

I began the chapter with this particular story because I want to emphasize the importance of the community as an essential element of how God works to bring people to Christ. There are plenty of examples of people coming to faith just through personal searching or through contact with only one or two believers, but those are exceptions to the rule. Most stories I am aware of are closer to Bill's. People *see* the gospel in the way Christians relate to one another and in the way they serve, and then they *hear* the gospel in a welcoming environment. The opposite effect is also true, unfortunately. When the Christian community is dysfunctional or very unwelcoming to strangers, the gospel itself never gets a hearing. Jesus' prayer for the unity of believers is very telling here—"that all of them may be one, Father, just as you are in me and I am in you. May they also be in us *so that the world may believe that you have sent me*" (John 17:21).

Take another look at Bill's experience. He became aware of a void in his life, but no answers began to appear until he recalled that visit to the church group in Dallas that both welcomed him and included him in a project of mercy. Then after a season of personal searching that only deepened his sense of need, the Lord sent a Christian housemate who invited Bill to another church. In that setting Bill was slowly absorbing the truth of the gospel and at the same time experiencing a sense of belonging that he found irresistible. Bill laughs when he recalls how important the invitations to brunch were in his first steps, but that points out the importance of hospitality in the welcome extended to people who are searching. It was in the church setting that Bill was converted and confessed Christ publicly. The season of growth and involvement in ministry followed very naturally because he was already part of a Christian community. This is not to say that Bill has not had personal struggles and periods of doubt, but there was always a safe place, his church, during those difficult times.

I used the term *Christian community* rather than *church* because I recognize that there are many examples of the Spirit working outside the organized church. These may be Christian evangelistic ministries or informal groups at work or in homes. The principle of community is a critically important element of God's work in people's lives, however it is expressed. Even groups that concentrate on personal evangelism will typically have groups where people can come as their interest in spiritual matters grow.

I have recently been taking an informal poll in churches when I speak on this subject. I ask members of the congregation to raise a hand either to indicate that their coming to faith was more of a personal quest or to indicate that they came to faith in a community or family setting where they saw the gospel in others in the process of hearing the gospel explained. Without making a formal count, it has appeared to me that about 90 percent of the hands were raised to indicate that people came to faith in the context of a community of believers. Recent writings on reaching out to the postmodern world make the point that we must draw people into community to be effective.[1] I agree

1. See *Total Church: A Radical Reshaping around Gospel and Community* by Tim Chester and Steve Timmis (Wheaton, IL: Crossway, 2008).

but would say that this is nothing new. Even though the matter of personal witness has been constantly stressed, in reality that personal witness becomes particularly effective when it includes bringing people into a setting where they are witnesses to Christ among his people.

It is my observation that the healthiest form of evangelism is linked to a local church. Within the church there may be smaller groups to which a seeker can relate, such as in the example of Kathy mentioned earlier. One of the frustrations of ministries that obtain lots of "decisions for Jesus" is that so few of those who make such decisions actually follow through. But perhaps those decisions are just the first steps in an authentic conversion. Those people need a place to grow at the pace God has for them, and that should be a welcoming and nurturing congregation of the followers of Jesus. Of course, that becomes a challenge to all of our churches. The tendency of churches to become ingrown and unwilling to welcome the "unwashed" is a constant area for growth. But the congregation that gathers weekly to worship and study and is made up of multiple generations and people at all stages of spiritual growth is the ordinary place the Lord has designed for bringing new life into the world.

The church is also the Christian community to which the sacraments of baptism and Communion have been given. There can be no doubt that these have been frequently abused and separated from their true meaning. Baptism, however, is the fundamental means of a person identifying with Christ and his people. This is mentioned over and over in Scripture and is an essential part of the conversion of those coming from outside the church. (The situation of those raised *in* the church will be the subject of chapter 13.) Communion is the fundamental means of expressing continued dependence on Christ along with others who have the same conviction. The bread bears witness to the body of Jesus, who came to earth for us, and the wine pictures the shedding of his blood for our forgiveness. We don't just look at these symbols—we actually take them in, and we do this *with* our Christian family. What a wonderful picture of believing the gospel and living for Christ.

As important as this principle is in a Western setting, it is even more important in cultures where family and community have a higher value than the individual. In an earlier chapter I told the story of the conversion of Mr. U (after a sixty-five-year spiritual pregnancy!) and his children. The church where they finally came to confess their faith is in London, but it ministers to a very diverse population, mostly South Asians. That church has a vision for ministry that is built around the importance of providing a place of belonging for any who come. Bob Heppe, the team leader, constantly reminds his fellow workers that *people need to be "belongers" before they become believers*, and they try to practice this in the way they "do church." Anyone who attends is welcome to be part of all that goes on. Each weekly service includes a vegetarian meal to respect the Hindus who may come, and events during the week are always open to the community. This is a good example of what is called today a *missional* congregation.

AN APPLICATION

When Bill described being asked to open up a Bible in the church service, he was referring to a practice that I have followed for years and that has proven to be helpful to people with little or no background in church or the Bible. It is simply a matter of helping people find where to read in the Bible by citing the page number and then actually waiting for people to look up the text. I try to confine my preaching largely to the main text rather than asking people to jump from place to place in the Bible. The actual content of the message can still be for the whole congregation, but once the Bible is open, people are more able to consider its meaning at various levels of understanding because they can read it for themselves.

There are other ways to be helpful to those unfamiliar with the Bible, but my preference is to encourage people to actually open a Bible. This will be a new experience for many of them, and once it becomes more familiar they can begin to do Bible reading in other settings. With an open Bible it is not uncommon for people to find themselves reading ahead or focusing on other parts of the text than what I happen to be preaching from. This can be a very good thing, and the Spirit can make Scripture come alive in ways that transcend our abilities to explain them. These people are sitting in the midst of a community whose cornerstone is Jesus himself, where God lives by his Spirit (Eph. 2:19–22), and where they are opening a Spirit-given Book to hear the Word of God explained. This is a unique environment where God can speak to hearts and draw men, women, and children to himself.

CHAPTER 6

Charles Colson: A Case Study of Regeneration and Conversion

I WAS A PASTOR in the Washington, DC, area when the conversion of Charles Colson was front-page news. I still remember reading the lengthy interview with him in the *Washington Post* with great skepticism—until I came to the final question. The interviewer asked what had changed since Mr. Colson's "born-again experience." His reply, as I recall, was this: "My whole view of the world has changed, and particularly the realization that Washington is not the center of true power. There are other things more important and significant." On reading that, I was convinced that Charles Colson was a profoundly changed man. He did not focus on an experience or feelings but on a new way of looking at life.

Chuck began Prison Fellowship soon after serving a prison term when he pled guilty for his role in the illegal use of classified materials from the Pentagon (not for the scandal known as Watergate, as is frequently assumed). At first the ministry consisted largely of bringing groups of Christian prisoners to Washington. It was my privilege to be part of those formative years of the ministry, to be the pastor of several of the staff, and to participate in many of the early events. With God's blessing, Prison Fellowship has expanded to become the international ministry it is today.

Chuck's first book, *Born Again*, is a spiritual autobiography that tells of his background, Washington years, conversion, and prison experience. It is still very worthwhile reading even if the political events are several decades old. Thanks to this book I can tell Chuck's story using his own words. They were written soon after he came to faith and therefore represent his early reflections on the work of God in his heart. Included in Chuck's story is another story—that of the friend who first spoke to him about Christ.

Chuck's first awareness of the calling work of the Spirit came from a visit to the Boston office of an old college friend and prospective client, Tom Phillips. At the time of their visit Tom was president of Raytheon Corporation, and Chuck was returning to a career in law after several years as Special Counsel to President Nixon. Before entering the office, Chuck was actually warned by an aide that Tom had been through a religious experience and he shouldn't be surprised if he tried to talk about it. What he found instead was a man radiating a sense of peace who was totally different from the Tom Phillips he had once known. Instead of getting right down to business, Tom asked Chuck how he was doing in a way that made it clear he was genuinely interested and wanted to be helpful. By the end of the conversation it was Chuck who asked Tom what had happened to him, and he heard Tom's confession that he had "accepted Jesus Christ." Without pressing the point, Tom simply told Chuck that if he would like to hear more of the story he would be very happy to tell him. Chuck left the office puzzled by the expression "accepted Jesus Christ" but knowing that Tom had something he needed, and he felt compelled to find an opportunity for further conversation.

That opportunity came several months later as Chuck and his wife, Patty, got away from Washington for a vacation in Maine. On the way they stopped near Boston to be with Chuck's parents, but he also found an excuse to slip away and visit with Tom. He had to learn why a man who was so obviously successful needed to accept Christ. He was welcomed by Tom and his wife, Gert, and the two men had a long conversation.

They began with Tom telling his story, punctuated by questions from Chuck. Tom spoke of an emptiness that would not go away in spite of all his earthly accomplishments. Finally, in desperation, he attended a crusade that Billy Graham was conducting at Madison Square Garden in New York City. He went out of curiosity and yet hoping he might find some answers. As he listened to Billy Graham he realized that the missing piece was a "personal relationship with Jesus Christ, the fact that I hadn't ever asked Him into my life."[1] That night Tom walked forward and gave his heart to Christ.

Chuck found himself totally mystified by the terminology his friend was using. They went on to talk for several hours, and Tom moved from telling his story to reading from the Bible and C. S. Lewis's book, *Mere Christianity*. This was all new and puzzling to Chuck, but Tom was very patient in answering his questions. After several hours of conversation Chuck brought the evening to a close saying, "Tom, you've shaken me up. I'll admit that. That chapter [the chapter on pride in *Mere Christianity*]

1. Charles W. Colson, *Born Again* (Old Tappan, NJ: Chosen Books, 1976), 110. Used with permission.

describes me. But I can't tell you I'm ready to make the kind of commitment you did. I've got to be certain. I've got to learn a lot more, be sure all my reservations are satisfied. I've got a lot of intellectual hangups to get past."[2]

Tom was very understanding, although he did throw Chuck into a panic by asking if they could pray to end the visit. Chuck agreed, but when he heard Tom actually "speaking directly and personally to God, almost as if he were sitting beside us," he didn't know how to respond. He finally left the house and got into his car. The sense of being drawn was overwhelming, and he started back into the house but noticed that they were turning off the lights and going upstairs. As Chuck pulled out of the driveway, tears were flowing uncontrollably. Finally Chuck pulled off and wept what he called "tears of relief."

> And then I prayed my first real prayer. "God, I don't know how to find You, but I'm going to try! I'm not much the way I am now, but somehow I want to give myself to You." I didn't know how to say more, so I repeated over and over the words: Take me.
>
> I had not "accepted" Christ—I still didn't know who He was. My mind told me it was important to find that out first, to be sure that I knew what I was doing, that I meant it and would stay with it. Only, that night, something inside me was urging me to surrender—to what or to whom I did not know.[3]

Notice Chuck's own comment about this experience. He said, "I had not 'accepted' Christ—I still didn't know who He was." He recognized that God was somehow moving into his life, and he offered up his first prayer, but he could only describe it

2. Ibid., 115.
3. Ibid, 116–17.

as "something inside me." Taken by itself, that kind of spiritual experience can mean anything, or perhaps it wasn't spiritual at all, but just an emotional release from all the pressure he was feeling. As we have seen in the study of the birthline, the fact that such undefined experiences are actually the work of the Spirit can only be determined by what is produced. When the Spirit calls, he calls us to wholehearted surrender to Christ. That is exactly what happened to Chuck Colson, as he goes on to describe.

In the next chapter of *Born Again*, "Cottage by the Sea," Chuck describes the experience that followed his encounter in front of the Phillipses' house. He and Patty continued their trip to the Maine community of Boothbay Harbor, where they stayed in an inn that looked out on the sea. They had a chance to relax, but Chuck could not escape the evening at the Phillipses' home. He and Patty actually discussed matters of faith and religion in a personal way for the first time in their marriage. He describes digging into the copy of *Mere Christianity* that Tom Phillips had given him and reading the Bible with new interest. He encountered Jesus Christ for the first time as he read about him in Lewis and in the Bible. All the thoughts that came to him he wrote on a pad of yellow legal paper, just as he did when preparing a court case. After several days of thoughtful reading and consideration he finally came to a place of decision. There was a compelling sense that he needed to "accept without reservations Jesus Christ as lord of my life." These are his words describing that decision:

> As something pressed that question home, less and less was I troubled by the curious phrase "accept Jesus Christ." It had sounded at first both pious and mystical, language of the zealot, maybe black magic stuff. But "to accept" means no more than

"to believe." Did I believe what Jesus said? If I did, if I took it on faith or reason or both, then I accepted. Not mystical or weird at all, and with no in between ground left. Either I would believe or I would not—and believe it all or none of it. . . .

And so early that Friday morning, words I had not been certain I could understand or say fell naturally from my lips: "Lord Jesus, I believe You. I accept You. Please come into my life. I commit it to You."

With these few words that morning came a sureness of mind that matched the depth of feeling in my heart. . . . God was filling the barren void I'd known for so many months, filling it to its brim with a whole new kind of awareness.[4]

It becomes very evident that the "something" moving him to surrender several days earlier was the calling of the Holy Spirit because as Chuck actually studied the gospel and the claims of Christ, he now found them more and more logical and compelling. A phrase like "accept Christ," which had totally baffled him at one point, now made perfectly good sense. He speaks again of "something" that "pressed that question home" with the clear implication that it was God bringing him to the place of decision. Chuck describes the common experience of one who is being drawn to Christ. While we are struggling with the call of God, all we know is that something outside of ourselves is stirring us to believe. It is only in looking back to interpret the experience that we appreciate the mysterious moving of the Holy Spirit. But when the Spirit works, we come to Christ.

In the end Chuck prayed simply and believed in Christ as Lord and Savior. This is *conversion*, as I have been defining it. It is a human response of faith and repentance to the inner call of

4. Ibid, 129–30.

the Spirit. Even in describing this moment, Chuck interpreted it as a return to the point when he tearfully prayed, "take me" on the road in front of the Phillipses' home.

> The search that began that week on the coast of Maine, as I pondered it, was not quite as important as I had thought. It simply returned me to where I had been when I asked God to "take me" in that moment of surrender on the little country road in front of the Phillips' home. What I studied so intently all week opened a little wider the new world into which I had already taken my first halting, shaky steps.[5]

He recognized, even as a new believer, that this second prayer of commitment was not *the* all-important moment but was another step along the path he had already started to walk. God had been there *first* drawing him, and now he was surrendering with much greater understanding than before.

Notice that he reports that words that were once alien to him now fell *naturally* from his lips. He even describes the fact that having prayed the prayer, there was a "sureness of *mind* that matched the depth of feeling in my *heart*" (emphasis mine). In other words, his inner man had already been transformed supernaturally, and he now made the choice that brought his mind into accord with his new nature.

This is a particularly dramatic example of how the new birth happened to one man. I hope by this point you have read enough stories to rejoice in how God worked in Charles Colson without feeling that you are missing out because you have had a different experience. In fact, Mrs. Colson, who witnessed her husband's conversion firsthand, has a strong testimony of trust

5. Ibid, 129.

in Christ that was part of her Roman Catholic upbringing. In a later book Chuck remarks that at first Patty was very upset by the insistence that she tell people exactly when she was born again. "Patty, like Ruth Graham and millions of others, cannot pinpoint a precise moment or sudden awakening. She grew up in a Christian home, always attended worship services, can never remember a moment when she didn't believe, and over the last thirty years has experienced an ever-deepening relationship with Christ."[6] That quotation comes from a chapter entitled "The Sin of Presumption" and includes Chuck's observations as a mature believer about the nature of conversion. He says, "There is a great difference between a humanly induced 'decision' and a true conversion, the new birth of the Spirit. Conversion is a process that begins with God's regenerating work—an instant when the Spirit gives life—and continues as we grow through the process of sanctification."[7]

6. Charles Colson and Ellen Vaughn, *Being the Body* (Nashville: W Publishing Group, 2003), 60.
7. Ibid, 62.

CHAPTER 7

What Is a Spiritual Midwife?

IN THE FIRST PART of the book we looked at the new birth. I introduced the concept of the birthline as a tool to help understand how we actually experience new birth. We then looked carefully at Jesus' conversation with Nicodemus in John 3 to get a foundation for interpreting our experience. I asked you to consider your own story in greater depth than perhaps you have done before, and I told the stories of several others to demonstrate what spiritual birth looks like.

Almost invariably when I present the birthline I find the discussion moving from people's consideration of their own experience to how that applies to their involvement with others. That is what the second part of this book is all about. The statement I frequently make is this: *We are not called to be salesmen for Jesus, trying to close the "deal" no matter what it takes; we are called to be midwives, available and ready to help with the birth.*

Midwifery is an ancient and honorable profession in which ordinary people are given enough skill to help mothers with the birth of their children. Today there are full-time midwives, but for most of history they were women who cared for their own homes and families, yet were always available to the community when a new baby was on the way. Whether or not you are in "full-time" ministry, I want to give you the basics that will equip you to be as helpful as possible when a new baby is on the way. This, in my mind, is the work of a spiritual midwife. God is the one who is actually bringing about the new life. But he uses people like us to help with the birth and growth of that new life.

A number of years ago I was invited to be a speaker at a gathering of missionaries. One of the other speakers was a physician who had specialized for years in the health problems of missionary children. It was clear from his speaking that he knew what he was talking about. At one point during one of his talks, he interrupted himself and commented that although he was speaking in generalities, he was drawing his conclusions based on years of actual cases that he had seen.

That remark struck a chord with me, and I recall thinking to myself that this was precisely what I was trying to do in understanding just how people come to faith in Christ. I was learning to listen carefully, to ask the right kind of questions, and to take the time necessary to at least have a sense of where a person was in his or her spiritual journey. And just like the doctor whose remark caught my attention, I was discovering that the more cases I dealt with in this way, the more I was able to see how the fundamental principles of biblical truth fit into the lives of those with whom I was working.

Before we get to the particulars of serving as spiritual midwives, consider two preliminary concepts that came from those remarks from the doctor. The first is the importance of learning to listen, including the skill of asking key questions. The second concept comes from the reference to cases.

LEARNING TO LISTEN

Think about your first visit to any skilled practitioner, whether a doctor, a psychologist or counselor, a financial advisor, a consultant—or a midwife. They have a good idea of what is healthy or sound, but they need to know where you are and how to apply their particular expertise to your situation. They will start by asking key questions, and then, after listening carefully to your responses, they ask other questions that help clarify your situation. This is not just passive listening but drawing out of you information and insights that dig deeper than perhaps you had thought about before. And slowly, based on both careful listening and his knowledge of his field of expertise, the counselor will begin to offer observations and then conclusions. This kind of listening is a skill, and without it the most expert knowledge can be misapplied. That is why most of us prefer to talk to men or women who have experience in working with people as well as textbook knowledge. We want to know we have been *heard* before we listen to what they have to tell us.

I am not necessarily advocating doing interviews at the level of formality that I just described (although that can be done too), but I am trying to remind you of how important it is to know how to listen. Let me reemphasize that we need to know the "textbook," the teaching of the Bible, as our foundation. Before we actually apply that teaching, however, we need to try to understand where people are and what kind of questions they are asking. Think of how wrong it would be for a doctor to write out a prescription to cure a particular condition before he knew what the problem really was. The first issue, then, is an awareness of how important it is to listen.

In the matter of people's spiritual progress, we listen because we genuinely care for people and want to be part of God's work in their lives. Our listening can't be just a polite pause before we launch into our witness. Perhaps a person is just getting started and wants to know a basic question about God, but because we haven't really listened, we decide to give a total gospel presentation. That is certainly what is ultimately needed, but are they ready for it yet? We will only know because we take some time to ask questions and listen.

We also need to keep in mind that people are far more interested in listening to what we have to say if they are receiving answers to questions *they* are asking. In the example of Philip and the man from Ethiopia (Acts 8), Philip was sensitive enough to understand what the man was struggling with and asked simply, "Do you understand what you are reading?" (v. 30). At that point the man *invited* Philip to help him understand. (We will consider this case in detail in chapter 8.) Study Jesus' encounter with the woman at the well of Samaria (John 4), and notice how skillful he was in helping her ask questions that he then answered in ways that brought her to faith.

THE EXPERIENCE OF BETTY

I still remember one of the first times I presented the birthline to a group of prisoners who had been brought to our city by Prison Fellowship. As we were talking about the implications of spiritual birth as a process in terms of how we relate to others, I was interrupted by an enthusiastic woman named Betty. She described how she had come to faith in Christ after her incarceration and then how she zealously tried to get all those in jail with her to also believe. She told our group that after a while people kept away from her, and she realized she might be doing more harm than good. So she decided that she would pray for people, be a servant to those in her cellblock, and wait on God to work. Not long after that decision, a fellow prisoner approached her and said she was having trouble sleeping. Betty said she was immediately tempted to tell her that her problem was she needed her sins forgiven and needed Jesus to be her Savior. But, Betty told us, that was not what the woman asked for—she needed help in getting to sleep; so she pointed her to a psalm she could read before going to bed. That night the woman not only had a peaceful night's rest, but she woke up to find a ray of the sun shining on the Bible that she had been reading in bed. Was this a sign? Who can say? But it grabbed the woman's attention, and she had a sense of God moving in her life.

She came to Betty with another question, and with a very teachable spirit. Betty said, "You know what I did? I answered her question and let her know I was open anytime she wanted to talk. And the next time she came back to talk I just took things as far as she wanted to go. Now, with what you have been explaining, I have a sense of what might be happening. I can't wait to go back and see where this will go. If this is God at work in her heart, she will come to Jesus. But if the time isn't right, I don't want to force her into something that isn't real."

CASE STUDIES

The second basic concept in the matter of being a spiritual midwife is the value of case studies. In any helping profession, there is a common practice of taking the model that comes from the textbook (of a healthy body, a solid marriage, an effective business, or whatever) and then illustrating it with numerous real-world experiences that are called *cases* or *case studies*. The cases never fit the model exactly, but the more various cases are studied, the more people become comfortable with starting with the model and adapting it to different situations.

Every story included in this book could also be called a case study. In the previous chapter I put the case studies of Charles Colson and Tom Phillips side by side. They are two different stories but illustrate the same model. I am trying to give enough pictures of how the new birth is actually experienced so that you will begin to develop skill in discerning what is happening in the people you are working with. It is important to remember that we are dealing with something supernatural and invisible, so we can never say with absolute certainty that we know what God is doing. But because the work of the Spirit in the heart results in changed lives, we can learn something of what that looks like in various cases.

The idea of doing spiritual case studies is not a new idea. One of the most important books in the history of Christianity in America is a little book by Jonathan Edwards called *A Faithful Narrative of the Surprising Work of God* (1736). It is a story of the revival that came to Edward's town of Northampton, Massachusetts, but a large part of the book gives case studies of particular conversion experiences and Edwards's analysis of them. A century later a Presbyterian pastor and scholar, Archibald Alexander, wrote a book entitled *Thoughts on Religious Experience*,[1] in which he not only gives a very thoughtful discussion of the various ways

---

1. Archibald Alexander, *Thoughts on Religious Experience* (1844; repr., London: Banner of Truth Trust, 1967).

people experience new birth but constantly illustrates his points with "cases." Both Edwards and Alexander treat the examination of cases as the normal thing to do. This is a long-neglected aspect of pastoral ministry. It was reading Alexander that introduced me to the older idea of the pastor as "physician of the soul."

For several years I have been assigning case studies as part of my teaching of the new birth and conversion. In more formal classroom settings, these are to be written up following a fairly fixed form and turned in as part of the student's grade. I am including two of those case studies in this chapter. You will note that they briefly introduce the person they interviewed, then summarize the interview, and end with observations of what was learned in doing the case study. I hope you will read them not only as interesting stories but with a view that you will be doing your own cases, whether or not they are formally written up.

The response of my students to this assignment has almost always been very positive. They actually approach people and ask if they would be willing to be interviewed to help with the class assignment. But then the conversation typically gets into a depth of examination that is only partially reflected in the written summary. Many times the persons interviewed express thanks for the opportunity to look at their spiritual pilgrimage in a way they had never done before. In a few instances the interview revealed that the person was not yet a believer but was ready to put his or her trust in Christ. So this assignment has been the door of conversion for some. And I have had many students, most of whom are pastors, thank me for introducing them to a means of having more in-depth conversations with people about their spiritual lives than they have ever had before. Years after taking my class I have had students tell me that studying the birthline and doing the case studies have fundamentally changed the way they do pastoral ministry.

Whether or not you are a pastor, I hope you will take these two ideas of careful listening and evaluating different cases and let them affect how you work with others. If the pastor is the *physician*, than the rest of us can be *midwives*. That means we have enough skill to be sensitive to where people are and help in the birth, but we also know when it is time to call on the doctor for the more challenging cases.

TWO CASE STUDIES (FROM FORMER STUDENTS)

Case Study of Sivaraman V.

Introduction. Sivaraman, or "Siva" for short, was born in Madras, India. Raised as a Hindu in the Brahman caste, he faithfully attended to temple prayers and spent hours praying to the Hindu gods. In fact, Siva's name is a tribute to two Hindu gods—Siva and Raman. Needless to say, this man was steeped in Hinduism from the earliest age.

Narrative. Though devoted to a different religion, Siva indicates that his spiritual disciplines of prayer and temple worship created a godward orientation and an awareness of spiritual things that would ultimately stimulate an interest in Christianity. Siva was convinced as a small child that he was a sinner and participated in the common Hindu ritual of reading the Vedas (Hindu bible) and confessing his depravity before the gods. This assumption of his sinfulness became important as he left his homeland at the age of twenty-two and traveled to the United States to attend graduate school.

Upon arriving at school, Siva met a fellow Indian who was a Christian. This relationship proved to be a vital means of grace in the Lord's effectual call. Ivan, Siva's new Christian friend, was also from Madras and had already crossed the cultural and religious chasm that Siva would ultimately confront. Ivan became a strong and consistent voice for the gospel in Siva's life.

Evidences of effectual calling abound in Siva's story. After finishing school, Siva relocated only to have Ivan, in God's providential mercy, relocate to the same area to work for the same business. Ivan soon found a good church and began to invite Siva to join him in various outings with the church folk. Siva reports, "One thing that struck me was that they (the people from church) accepted me. They would always call me to see if I wanted to join them. I can't think of any time I wasn't invited to join them." Siva found himself attracted to the life and vitality of these Christians while at the same time questioning his religious assumptions about Hinduism. Siva got involved out of loneliness, but he soon found himself drawn to their message.

Early religions impressions die slowly though, and Siva was far too superstitious to convert to Christianity just because he was attracted to it. He was a spiritual man, and he knew that religion was far more than just fun and fellowship. In fact, Siva remembered how the *pujari* (the Hindu equivalent of a pastor) had prayed over his brothers as they were smitten with yellow fever as kids. The boys' recovery was dramatic, and Siva left that experience convinced that there was real power in Hinduism. Therefore, a conversion to Christianity represented more than just a consumer swap of one religion for another. In Siva's mind, conversion would place his life and family at risk and alienate him from his entire caste. The cost was great.

Siva attended the Christian church for nine months and listened intently to the preaching. Attracted, yet still unpersuaded, he arrived at a crossroads where he felt he needed to make a decision but lacked the heart substance to decide for Christ. Shortly thereafter, Siva had a life-altering vision. In it, Jesus came to him and bid him to come. Siva's response was utter fear. Hindus were familiar with visions, and they were always a bad omen of future calamity.

The vision prompted Siva to stop attending church and to turn from this Christian foolishness. The vision left him scared and confused. Then, several days later, Siva's sacred thread broke while taking a shower. The sacred thread is the covenant sign of one's Hindu faith. If it breaks, one's connection with his god is compromised, and it is believed that the father of the thread's owner is also in jeopardy.

Siva was distraught and cried out to every god he could imagine. In this time of desperate prayer, the vision of Jesus returned with more power and clarity. As the vision subsided, Siva felt a revelation and faith regarding the person and work of Jesus Christ spring to life. In that moment he submitted his life to Christ and was converted. Siva says, "In that instant, I recognized that Jesus was the only way!"

Concluding Observations. This happened twelve years ago. Since that time, Siva has walked faithfully with Christ, confessed his faith before his Hindu family, married an American woman, and became father to two boys. He now leads a ministry helping internationals understand and apply the gospel of Jesus Christ.

Siva's story is a remarkable testimony to God's activity prior to conversion. Be it his spiritual orientation as a Hindu, his experiences with spiritual power, his providential relationship with Ivan, his involvement in a church prior to conversion, or his dramatic visions of Jesus Christ, it is evident that God was at work long before Siva responded to him. It is also evident that Siva needed the supernatural experience of a heavenly vision in conversion to break the powerful grip of Hinduism over his life.

God brought Siva thousands of miles to expose him to the gospel. Siva's life is a remarkable testimony to preparatory grace and a great reminder of the effort God exerts to prepare us for the gospel. God's pursuit of Siva now motivates Siva's pursuit of other internationals. As an object of grace, he has now become a means of grace. Praise be to God![2]

Case Study of Joyce

Introduction. Joyce is a member of our congregation and the mother of three children.

Narrative. Joyce's father was Jewish and her mother Roman Catholic. She was brought up in the Jewish faith and was very active in synagogue worship. At age thirteen she had her *bat mitsvah*. In deference to her mother's faith, her father would allow Joyce to celebrate Christmas and other traditional Christian holidays. After her parents divorced, she stayed with her father and stepmother, who was Protestant, and was brought up by them. As a result, she was even allowed to attend a church camp one summer, where she was exposed to the existence of the New Testament along with other basic truths. To her, it became more and more a mystery why Jews, who believe the Old Testament, would not accept the New Testament as well.

2. Thanks to Dr. David Harvey for permission to use this case study.

At school she would be taunted sometimes by her school-mates, who warned her that she would go to hell if she did not believe in Jesus. Going through a time of rebellion against her father, she started defiantly wearing a cross, which made him very upset. Again, she could not understand why her father would be so offended by her wearing the symbol of Christianity. At age eighteen she moved out of her parents' home and, while in college, attended a Brethren church, where she took part in a Bible study. Even after she married, she was still ignorant of the truth. After the birth of her first child, she started looking for another church because she definitely did not want to bring up her daughter in the Jewish faith and also because she had many questions of her own. She was hungry and thirsty for knowledge about the Bible and about the truth.

She was invited to our church through one of our members and started attending with the hope that she could find answers to her many questions. These had to do with the relationship between the Old Testament and the New Testament, between Judaism and Christianity, and especially with the apostle Paul, who himself converted from Judaism to Christianity, and, of course, with Jesus himself. I remember lending her my copy of *The Life and Times of Jesus the Messiah* by Alfred Edersheim, which she read with great interest.

During that time, Joyce was invited to be part of our "A Call to Joy" program, a one-on-one mentoring program in which she started meeting with her mentor, Sharon, on a regular basis. At their first meeting, Sharon explained the gospel by means of the "Bridge Illustration" and subsequently led Joyce to confess her sin and receive Christ as Lord and Savior when she was ready for it. There was great rejoicing in heaven and in our church at the time. She was then baptized, together with her daughter, and was received into the membership of the church. She has become actively involved in Bible study, in teaching Sunday school, and in reading books about the faith.

Concluding Observations. Joyce has the privilege to be able to point to a very precise moment in her life when she converted to Christ. Her new birth was evident to all of us, as we were observing her and fervently praying for her at the time. Yet it is quite clear that the Lord was at work in her life and in her heart from a very early time on.

She responded with great interest to my presentation of the birthline and fully agreed that the Lord was working in her life even while she was still actively involved in Judaism. This is why learning about the life of the apostle Paul was so important and of such great help to her, since he had followed a similar path. The very fact that she had no peace until her many, many questions were answered shows that the Holy Spirit was inwardly preparing her to respond outwardly to the preaching of the gospel in the church. It was also in God's providence that Joyce should be mentored by a woman who loves the Lord and who has a wonderful gift of evangelism, enabling her to start a conversation and gently lead people to consider matters of eternal consequence for their own lives.[3]

---

3. Thanks to Dr. Charles Winkler for permission to use this case study.

CHAPTER 8

Studies in Scripture: The Ministry and Teachings of Paul

IN CHAPTER 3 we looked carefully at Jesus' conversation with Nicodemus to establish a biblical basis for our discussion of how we experience the new birth. In the same way we must let Scripture direct how we conduct ourselves in helping others to know that same experience. The Scripture is clear that while God is the one who works, he uses the message of the gospel and the love and involvement of others to accomplish his mysterious work of changing hearts. The supreme example of a man who was conscious of how God worked in this way was the apostle Paul. He described God's work of salvation in his own heart in this way: "God . . . set me apart from birth, and *called me by his grace*" (Gal. 1:15). In defining his ministry he told the Corinthians:

> What, after all, is Apollos? And what is Paul? Only servants, through whom you came to believe—as the Lord has assigned

to each his task. I planted the seed, Apollos watered it, but God made it grow. So neither he who plants nor he who waters is anything, but only God, who makes things grow. (1 Cor. 3:5–7)

The two passages that follow should be studied in the same way we considered John 3. The apostle Paul described what was going on as he and others preached the gospel. This is more than a historical record—the power of the Spirit is still at work as we try to speak of Christ.

1 CORINTHIANS 1:17—2:5

1: [17]For Christ did not send me to baptize, but to preach the gospel—not with words of human wisdom, lest the cross of Christ be emptied of its power.

[18]For the message of the cross is foolishness to those who are perishing, but to us who are being saved it is the power of God. [19]For it is written:

"I will destroy the wisdom of the wise;
　　the intelligence of the intelligent I will frustrate."

[20]Where is the wise man? Where is the scholar? Where is the philosopher of this age? Has not God made foolish the wisdom of the world? [21]For since in the wisdom of God the world through its wisdom did not know him, God was pleased through the foolishness of what was preached to save those who believe. [22]Jews demand miraculous signs and Greeks look for wisdom, [23]but we preach Christ crucified: a stumbling block to Jews and foolishness to Gentiles, [24]but to those whom God has called, both Jews and Greeks, Christ the power of God and the wisdom of God. [25]For the foolishness of God is wiser

than man's wisdom, and the weakness of God is stronger than man's strength.

[26]Brothers, think of what you were when you were called. Not many of you were wise by human standards; not many were influential; not many were of noble birth. [27]But God chose the foolish things of the world to shame the wise; God chose the weak things of the world to shame the strong. [28]He chose the lowly things of this world and the despised things—and the things that are not—to nullify the things that are, [29]so that no one may boast before him. [30]It is because of him that you are in Christ Jesus, who has become for us wisdom from God—that is, our righteousness, holiness and redemption. [31]Therefore, as it is written: "Let him who boasts boast in the Lord."

2:[1]When I came to you, brothers, I did not come with eloquence or superior wisdom as I proclaimed to you the testimony about God. [2]For I resolved to know nothing while I was with you except Jesus Christ and him crucified. [3]I came to you in weakness and fear, and with much trembling. [4]My message and my preaching were not with wise and persuasive words, but with a demonstration of the Spirit's power, [5]so that your faith might not rest on men's wisdom, but on God's power.

Introduction

Our study of John 3 and *regeneration* clearly laid the foundation that it is the Holy Spirit who must change the heart. But Scripture is also very clear that the *instrument* or *tool* the Spirit uses in that transforming work is the preaching of the gospel. The passage quoted above is a very careful explanation by the apostle Paul of how the gospel actually works in the salvation of those who are alienated from God.

In addition to references to the gospel, the key word to pay attention to is *called* or *calling*. The word can be used in a number of ways, depending on the purpose behind the calling. In 1 Corinthians 1:1, for example, Paul was "called" to be an apostle. But he frequently used the word to speak of the inner work of God in drawing us to Christ. In several of his letters Paul begins by reminding his readers that they were believers and were in the church of Jesus Christ because they had experienced the call of God. "God, who has called you into fellowship with his Son Jesus Christ our Lord, is faithful" (1 Cor. 1:9). (See this also in Romans 1:6–7 and Galatians 1:6, 15 and in Peter's use of the word in 2 Peter 1:3, 10.)

It will become clear as you study the passage that Paul was zealous to fulfill his mission to preach Christ crucified. But he also understood that apart from the inward calling of God, his words would fall on deaf ears. If you want to understand the background of Paul's initial ministry to the Greek city of Corinth, read Acts 18:1–11.

Study of the Passage

Read through the passage at least twice. Pay particular attention to references to the *gospel* (either the word itself or phrases such as *Christ crucified*), *power*, and *called*.

Now notice some of the details of the passage.

1:17. Paul makes it clear that his particular ministry was that of missionary/evangelist—one who proclaims the gospel to begin the church—rather than one who stays and builds the church (a pastor who baptizes and nurtures). But in the context of the intellectual Greeks and critical Jews, who formed the initial core of the Corinthian church, he felt the need to explain why the gospel is so powerful. The key is to give a

94

straightforward presentation of the person of Christ and the work he did on the cross.

1:18–23. Paul is quite clear that it is no accident that the gospel—the message of Christ crucified—does not appeal to human intellect. God has actually *designed* the gospel so that it offends both human reason (the Greeks and the Gentile world in general) and human sensitivities (the Jews' regard for their Messiah). The result of that upside-down action of God, making the world's wisdom foolishness and its idea of foolishness to be true wisdom, is so that those who come to salvation will realize that it was not because they were so wise or clever to figure it all out. The dilemma, however, is, *who will come to salvation?* No one wants it, whether they are Gentiles or Jews! They might have been desperately searching for God and a way out of their situations, just as many are today, but when they heard God's solution—the gospel—they were unanimous that it *couldn't* be the right answer.

1:24–25. The word "but" that begins verse 24 is the critical hinge word of the passage and is the key to understanding how the gospel works. Paul understood that as he proclaimed a message ridiculed and rejected by all, something hidden was going on. Among those who came across his path, including both Gentiles and Jews, were some whose hearts were being prepared and stirred from within. They were those whom God was *calling*, and for them that message of supposed foolishness was a balm to their souls. They were discovering in a personal way the power of God and the wisdom of God. In all likelihood their first encounters with Paul or other gospel preachers had stirred animosity. Or perhaps, as seemed to be the case with many

"God-fearing Gentiles," hearts had already been prepared for the gospel, and they came to faith very quickly (Acts 13:26, 48).

The clear point of the text is that while the gospel message is true whether or not it is believed, it requires a powerful moving of God to make that gospel message come alive to a listener. We will discuss the implications of the text below, but for now just take in what it says.

1:26–31. These verses emphasize the truth that the gospel works because God makes it work. In verse 26 Paul asks them to "think of what you were when you were *called.*" It is a common approach of Paul to ask his readers to stop and remember where they were before coming to Christ (see 1 Cor. 6:9–11; Titus 3:3–7).[1] They needed to appreciate that there was nothing about them that would deserve what God has done for them in uniting them spiritually to Christ. Ultimately the reason we are *in Christ Jesus*, with the unimaginable blessings that come through him, is that this is what God has chosen to do. God *chose* to save people in the manner that he did so that all glory and boasting would be directed where it belongs—to the Lord.

2:1–5. The final portion of this passage makes it clear that Paul understood that the power to change lives was a supernatural one. It was the power of God—specifically, power that came from the Holy Spirit. The rest of the chapter has more to say about the working of the Holy Spirit in bringing us to a greater knowledge of God.

1. See my book, *The Walk: Steps for New and Renewed Followers of Jesus* (Phillipsburg, NJ: P&R Publishing, 2009), 83–107, where I identify the need to appreciate how we came to believe the gospel as the second step of gospel discipleship.

Implications of the Passage

In the birthline I have used the term *calling* to describe the concept of spiritual pregnancy. Whether or not that is precisely how Paul was using this word, he clearly taught that there is a time when people begin to wrestle with their need, which in turn prepares them to hear the gospel, believe it, and find Christ to be fully sufficient. Anyone who is truly converted will have some sense of awareness that it was God who brought them to a place of trust in Christ.

The word *gospel* means an announcement of good news. Paul summarized the gospel as the message of "Christ . . . crucified." But while the actual gospel message can involve more than the crucifixion, it will always point people to Jesus Christ and to the need to believe in him. The passages actually defining the gospel speak of the person of Christ promised in the Old Testament, as well as the key events of his life, death, and resurrection (Rom. 1:1–4; 1 Cor. 15:1–8). So every presentation of the gospel may not tell every aspect of the story, but if it is the gospel preached according to Scripture, it will inevitably point a person to Christ.

We should not be surprised when people are totally uninterested in the gospel message. This is the natural human condition. Sometimes we are recruited for mission or evangelistic projects by being told that, unlike where we are living, if we go to a certain place, multitudes there can't wait to hear the gospel so they can believe. In my experience, that has not proved to be the case. But the good news is that the Holy Spirit *is* at work, and God has promised that multitudes of every tribe and language will come into the kingdom. There are times and places where the Spirit seems to be particularly at work. But apart from the calling work of the Spirit, don't expect that hearts are any different in another city or country than where you live.

The challenge is to stay focused on Jesus and not try to dream up ways to make the message of the gospel more palatable to unbelievers. That doesn't mean we try to be offensive or foolish, but the ultimate "foolishness" is the gospel itself, the strange idea that a man crucified could actually be a savior.

1 THESSALONIANS 1:1–10

[1]Paul, Silas and Timothy, To the church of the Thessalonians in God the father and the Lord Jesus Christ: Grace and peace to you.

[2]We always thank God for all of you, mentioning you in our prayers. [3]We continually remember before our God and Father your work produced by faith, your labor prompted by love, and your endurance inspired by hope in our Lord Jesus Christ.

[4]For we know, brothers loved by God, that he has chosen you, [5]because our gospel came to you not simply with words, but also with power, with the Holy Spirit and with deep conviction. You know how we lived among you for your sake. [6]You became imitators of us and of the Lord; in spite of severe suffering, you welcomed the message with the joy given by the Holy Spirit. [7]And so you became a model to all the believers in Macedonia and Achaia. [8]The Lord's message rang out from you not only in Macedonia and Achaia—your faith in God has become known everywhere. Therefore we do not need to say anything about it, [9]for they themselves report what kind of reception you gave us. They tell how you turned to God from idols to serve the living and true God, [10]and to wait for his Son from heaven, whom he raised from the dead—Jesus, who rescues us from the coming wrath.

Introduction

I selected this passage because it is another reference to the necessity of the Holy Spirit to make the gospel come alive in people's hearts. But this is also an important passage because it shows the link between the *preaching* of the gospel and the *living* of the gospel. It introduces the vital issue of relationship and compassion as essential to the work of spreading the gospel.

This was one of the first of Paul's letters. He wrote it shortly after his visit to the city of Thessalonica, recorded in Acts 17:1–9.

Study the Passage

Read the passage at least twice. To gain more of a sense of the quality of Paul's caring for them, read 1 Thessalonians 2:1–16.

Consider some of the specifics of the passage:

verses 1–3. Silas was Paul's companion on the second missionary journey. Timothy was the messenger who took the letter to the Thessalonians, but they knew him as part of Paul's team. It is important to note that Paul always traveled and evangelized with others. No doubt part of their witness as they went from place to place was the chance for the people to observe how these Christians related to one another.

Paul thanks God for their faith, love, and hope. These three qualities also appear in 1 Corinthians 13, the famous "love chapter," and also Colossians 1:3–5. This suggests that Paul regularly taught that new life in Christ brought forth these three expressions as the primary fruit of believing the gospel.

verses 4–6. How could Paul be certain that they were God's beloved, his chosen? He knew it because of the way the gospel had come to them. He spoke the words, but through the presence of the Holy Spirit there was power and conviction that changed their hearts. The reference to power may mean the "signs and wonders" that often accompanied the preaching of the apostles. But the point was that the presence of God was there, not just words, and even though there was opposition, the people believed and experienced the joy of the Holy Spirit.

An important part of the impact of the gospel was the life of Paul and his companions. "You became imitators of us and of the Lord" points to a consistent pattern as God uses the changed lives of others as a key part of making the gospel come alive.

verses 7–10. The changed lives of the Thessalonians in turn became an important part of their witness. It was not only the Word that sounded forth but their example. That example was of an authentic conversion—"you turned to God from idols" (faith and repentance)—and the new walk that follows conversion—"to serve the living and true God, and to wait for his Son from heaven."

Implications of the Passage

I'm not sure any of us could have the same level of spiritual discernment that Paul had and pronounce who is and who is not chosen of God. Nevertheless, I think it is possible to recognize times when the gospel is not welcome and other times when the Spirit seems to be making it real to people. We need to try to recognize when our words are falling on deaf ears and just stop. I can think of instances in which I have insisted on presenting the gospel, and the only discernible result has been that I never saw those people again. Perhaps the Lord still used my witness, but from my perspective I think it would have been wiser to wait until there was greater receptivity. Even when we are in a conversation with a stranger whom we may never see again, I don't think we help the cause of Christ by forcing them to listen when it is clear they don't want to. Pray that even a brief word or an act of kindness may serve as a seed that may begin to ripen later (1 Cor. 3:5–8).

A reading of the background of this passage in Acts 17 shows that Paul and his team were only in Thessalonica for a fairly brief time. That says to me that the quality of compassion does not require a long-term relationship. Effective gospel witness is not limited by a brief visit, but it does mean that we need to examine our hearts to see if we love people with the love of Jesus, and not simply as lost souls. In most settings this does call for cultivating genuine relationships over a period of time, but there can be exceptions to this rule. Jesus was certainly able to communicate love just by appearing on a scene, and we need to pray that we would have such hearts.

The lesson of the letter to the Thessalonian believers is the integration of a life lived in relationship and caring with the truth of the gospel. The familiar admonition of St. Francis ("Preach the gospel, and if necessary use words") has an element of truth, but in fact, the gospel *is* words. It is a message that people need to hear and believe. However, we must never lose sight of the fact that the gospel message gets far more attention when it is also demonstrated in changed lives.

I don't think that means we are supposed to do certain things "in order to be a testimony." When people perform in certain ways that they think unbelievers expect of Christians, it is just that—a performance. Everyone else is playing a role, and if we are playing the role of Christian to impress others, it will have the opposite effect. We need to be real people, and if we have been truly changed it will show.

TWO STORIES FROM SCRIPTURE

The New Testament not only gives us proper teaching about the work of God in our souls—it also records several examples of that happening. Luke, under the direction of the Holy Spirit, wrote about the early days of the church and included selected conversion stories. Just like the other stories we are reading, they describe particular experiences that are unique. Nevertheless we need to read them as a way to learn more about how God works.

The Story of the Ethiopian Official

Read Acts 8:26–39.

This man's heart was being prepared well before Philip appeared on the scene. He had been drawn to Jerusalem where he worshiped the one true God, and when Philip found him, he was reading the passage in the Bible that describes the brutal death of the one Isaiah called the servant of the Lord (Isa. 53). Perhaps our finding people who are seeking the Lord won't be quite as spectacular as Philip's experience, but we can still pray that God will give us what many call "divine appointments" to speak with people whose hearts have been prepared and who are ready to listen.

Notice that Philip asked questions at first. The result was that the Ethiopian man *invited* Philip to explain what the Scripture meant. Philip thoughtfully answered exactly what the man was asking for and then expanded the discussion to point the way to Christ. When God is calling, as is clearly the case here, we don't need to force people to listen. We listen to their questions and go from there.

We don't know how long this conversation took place or all that Philip said, but it ended with the man ready to confess his faith in Christ. Baptism was the definite symbol of his readiness to move from inquiry to actually being a follower of Jesus.

The Story of Cornelius

Read Acts 10:1–48.

In reading the story, keep in mind that this is not only the conversion of an individual (actually a household)—he is the first Gentile to be converted. This marks a major new step in the expansion of the kingdom. The coming of the Holy Spirit upon Cornelius and his household was a replay of the Day of Pentecost when the Spirit fell on the Jews (Acts 2), including speaking in tongues, and Peter had to be prepared for this through the giving of a vision. In chapter 11 he reports this to the church in Jerusalem and makes it clear that it is God who had opened this new door. But in addition to being a milestone of kingdom expansion, this is also a wonderful story of the conversion of a man and his household, which is how we will consider it.

This is the story of the conversion of a "good" person. He was a man who clearly saw his need, but it was more in the nature of a void in his life than conviction of particular evil acts. He was a *God-fearer,* which meant a Gentile who was seeking for truth, and he was known as a kind and generous man. But while Cornelius was a good person, he recognized that something was missing and was praying for whatever that might be to come to him. It is clear from reading the passage that Cornelius and his household were spiritually prepared to hear the gospel. What we read in Scripture is the climax of a process completed by their hearing and believing the gospel. Cornelius was not saved because he was a good and devout man, but because the Spirit opened his heart to Christ.

Peter had to overcome his own prejudices in order to present the gospel. We all have our assumptions about how God will work, and it is important that we not box God in. We need to learn to listen first, as Peter did, to get a sense of what God is already doing and then fit our conversation or presentation of the gospel to the situation. Be prepared to be surprised as you hear of the remarkable ways God gets through to people and brings them to a place where they are willing to hear the gospel.

CHAPTER 9

The Spiritual Midwife: Getting Started

ONE PERSON I KNOW shared the following experience:

Maria, twenty-five, approached me as I was performing temporary military chaplain duties at a naval base. Maria was engaged, and her particular concern was to find a minister who would conduct the service. When I asked her if she had approached the chaplains stationed at the base, she said, "They won't do it." When I asked why, she related a history of herself and her fiancé.

Maria was raised with no religious involvement. She remembered an occasional visit to church with friends, but she didn't recall any content, merely some of the buildings. Her fiancé's family was Mormon, but the parents had left the church some time ago and had no church affiliation at that time. Maria had no real understanding of God, nor did she understand why that is important to chaplains and local ministers, since "I only want to get married, not join their church."

When I presented the birthline illustration, she didn't understand what I was trying to say, nor could she describe clearly what she believed about God. In response to questions about God, faith, or personal commitment, she continued to reply, "I just don't know what I believe."

Since we had no basis for a conversation about God, having no understanding in common, I approached her particular question by asking her, "Maria, how many gods are there—one or more than one?" She replied, "Oh, there's only one God." "Good," I said. "We've narrowed the field of world religions to three. Christianity, Judaism, and Islam are the three great monotheistic religions of the world. What about Jesus, Maria? Was Jesus just a good person or moral teacher? Was Jesus a philosopher or prophet? Or was Jesus actually the Son of God?" "Oh, I believe that he's the Son of God," she said.

"Well then, Maria, we've just eliminated Islam and Judaism. What you're telling me is that you believe about Jesus as only Christians do." I then urged her to go to the nearest church off-base and listen for two weeks. If that one didn't suit her, I told her to go to another and so on until she found a church where she was able to understand what they were saying and enjoy the experience. In that search, I suggested, she could also find a pastor who would do her ceremony.

Maria is in the very beginning stages of religious inquiry. She doesn't have any negative feelings toward Christianity—she simply doesn't have any information or experience at all. The affirmation she can make—that there is one God and that Jesus is the Son of God—provides a place to plant and nurture seeds of faith. Her need is for a sensitive believer who will lead her to faith, answer her questions, and care for her.

This experience by one of my former students illustrates the fact that the birthline doesn't help in every situation. We need to remember that apart from the work of the Spirit we are "dead in [our] transgressions and sins" (Eph. 2:1). In once sense the birthline was helpful in that it gave my student a sense of where Maria was spiritually, but it wasn't close to a place where his work as a midwife would be needed. However, he did a good job of using the occasion to get her thinking more about spiritual issues.

The importance of effectively getting the gospel message out is a separate discussion. I mention several good resources in the For Further Reading section. There are any number of ways that God begins to move people toward faith—the influence of family and friends, literature tables, church or home groups for inquirers, casual conversations in the workplace, even personal tragedy and suffering. Furthermore, even before people take the slightest interest in the gospel, the secret work of the Spirit is preparing the heart in the earliest stages of the journey. We have already looked at several examples of what this can be like in actual experience.

The birthline is useful as a tool once people have become more serious about their relationship with God. It has been particularly valuable in helping people look back on their experience and celebrate the perseverance and mercy of God. But appreciating the *process* of the new birth has also proven helpful to people as they are coming to the place of conversion. Whether or not you actually draw out the birthline diagram for people, if you have it in your mind you will find that your conversations with them will focus on their progress toward conversion. By remembering God's patience with you, you will be content to let those you are working with move at their pace toward trusting Christ. At the same time you are able to point them toward the culmination of their spiritual pregnancy—a trust in Christ alone for eternal life. Knowing how to talk to people this way is especially important in ministry settings such as churches, Bible study groups, youth ministries, etc. where you see people on a continuing basis and you want them to feel free to continue coming to you to ask questions whenever they need to.

Take a moment to review the birthline, and notice particularly the earliest stages of the work of the Spirit.

PHYSICAL AND SPIRITUAL BIRTH

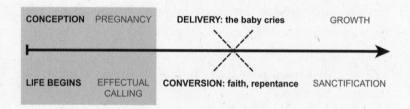

I have already explained how I present the idea of the new birth as the first lesson in a new members class. Since the people in the class have ordinarily been coming to the church for a while, most of them have an idea of what it means to be a follower of Christ. When I draw the dotted X and ask if they see themselves on the line, most will identify the fact that they are somewhere to the right of the X, which is to say they think of themselves as having been converted. But others have said to me that while they understand what I am saying, they know they are not yet converted, even though they feel drawn in that direction and almost feel it is inevitable that such a time will come. In such instances I tell people that *if* the Spirit is moving in their lives, they *will* come to a place where they freely submit themselves to

Christ and become his followers. I tell them that this may be a very dramatic moment or it may be very quiet, but in some way they will know in their hearts that they have come to believe.

Notice that I very deliberately use the word *if* when I try to describe to people how the Spirit works. Biblically it is clear that when it is God who is calling people, it will result in their trusting in Christ as Lord and Savior. Jesus said, "All that the Father gives me will come to me, and whoever comes to me I will never drive away. . . . No one can come to me unless the Father who sent me draws him. . . . My sheep listen to my voice; I know them, and they follow me. I give them eternal life, and they shall never perish; no one can snatch them out of my hand" (John 6:37, 44; 10:27–28).

I love to illustrate the call of God by picturing Jesus standing at the tomb of Lazarus and calling him to come out (John 11:43). I ask what would happen if we were standing there calling for Lazarus to come forth. The answer, of course, is that nothing would happen. But because it is Jesus calling, the power to respond comes with the call. When God calls, we come!

But while this is true, it is unwise to assume that we can be certain that we are seeing God at work, or perhaps more accurately, that we know just what God is doing in a person at the time we are talking to him or her. Human beings are made in the image of God, and although that image has been distorted by sin, it is not destroyed. Every person, therefore, has some level of spiritual hunger and can never escape a sense of having been created, despite his or her protestations to the contrary. In that sense all of us are spiritual. We should respect people's references to their spirituality, without assuming that means the Holy Spirit is in their lives. Jesus is clear that until the Spirit comes and changes the heart, there is no new birth, which means that people's inborn spirituality will not bring them to Christ. We can describe how God works but let the individual wrestle with how that relates to him or her personally.

Very recently a student who had just completed his work for my class stopped me to tell me a story. He told of working with a man in his congregation who started out as a casual visitor and had shown more and more interest in the things of God. Nick told me that his time in our class had given him a great desire to carefully listen and discern where the man was. They had conversations and Bible studies together, and eventually he used the birthline to explain to him how people come to faith. Nick told me that just a few weeks earlier, that man had come to him after a church service to say, "You know that line you showed me? Now there is an X on it!" Nick told me that what was particularly impressive to him was how seamlessly they were moving into what we typically call discipling. The new believer did not see his X as the end result but simply as an important step in the process of his spiritual pilgrimage.

START AT THE BEGINNING

When you are with people in a ministry setting, there will be opportunities to talk one on one. These are the best times to go into greater depth about where they see themselves in their spiritual journey. (The language of *journey* is familiar to many people and, like the birthline, conveys the idea of process.) This kind of quality time can come in the form of people coming for counseling or to talk about spiritual struggles. But it can also be the result of your taking the initiative and asking to meet for coffee or a meal to get better acquainted.

Usually the conversation will begin with either general chit-chat or what counselors call the presenting problem. In either case I look for an opportunity to ask the person I am with if he or she would mind taking some time for me to get a sense of his or her background. Most people, once a relationship is established, don't mind talking about their background, and this frequently serves to deepen the relationship, particularly as you add in certain elements of your own history. This is when the kind of active listening I described earlier is very important. Ask about their family and what kind of religious influence there was in the home. Ask about some of their earliest memories of thinking about God. If they describe a religious experience such as "I accepted Jesus when I was seven," ask for more detail. Take the time to walk through their lives up to the present. In many cases a striking pattern of God's work will emerge. I have often been able to point out to people evidences of God's gracious protection and the moving of the Spirit that they had not seen before. In some situations it becomes very helpful to actually describe the process of the new birth and conversion and even draw the birthline on a piece of paper. But the key is to listen thoughtfully through the asking of questions.

The more conversations you have like this, the more comfortable you will become. And because these are conversations about the work of the Spirit in people's lives, you will gain a sense of awe that you are part of what God is doing in someone's life. I have found that this approach moves people from their "duty to witness" to a sense of privilege that God is using us in his work.

During our stay in Spain to work on this book, Sandy and I took a few days to get away and visit with Christian friends who are working in a church in a different part of the country. As we were chatting together, one of the newer attendees dropped by, and in the process of getting acquainted she inquired about what sort of a book I was writing. I told her, and that prompted conversation from others there about their experiences in coming to faith. All agreed that it was much more of a process than a moment even though the couple with whom we were visiting had very definite points of conversion. I noticed that everyone was talking except the woman who had asked the original question. So I simply said to her, "Deborah, what was your religious background?" For the next several minutes, helped along by a few encouraging questions, she told us the story of her family's church background, her pilgrimage toward a more serious consideration of Christ, and something of her present situation. Later our friends told us that they had learned more about this woman through that conversation than they had ever known before.

There was one question I asked that they felt was particularly helpful in allowing the guest to speak about her faith. When I learn that people have come from a more traditional and conservative church background, such as Roman Catholicism or an Orthodox church, I remind them of the basics of what they have grown up with (God as Father, Son, and Holy Spirit; Jesus born of a virgin who died for our sins; etc.). Then I ask, "I know you have always believed this, but is there a time when all of this began to become *personal* for you?" In many cases people with this kind of background have totally rejected the church of their childhood, but in other instances they have not but sense something is lacking. In some cases people describe what amounts to a conversion experience even though their tradition doesn't use that kind of terminology. This question allows them to describe their pilgrimage without assumptions on our part about where their hearts are. In this case Deborah had great respect for her parents' church and agreed with the teachings as much as she understood them, but she was also in the process of coming to a more personal experience of Christ.

AN INTERVIEW WITH AMY AND COLLEEN

A colleague in ministry, Paul Miller, has been one of those who have encouraged me to write this book. Paul has developed a series of studies on the person of Jesus for use with people who have little or no background in church or biblical teaching. As members of the groups become more engaged with the material of the lessons, it often happens that some of them feel personally drawn to Jesus himself.

The following is an interview Paul did with two women who were in one of his studies.[1] It is a good illustration of how God uses the gospel message to call people to himself, but it is also a good example of how to use thoughtful questions to guide people to a greater understanding of their spiritual journey.

Q. What had your spiritual journey been like prior to coming to the Person of Jesus study?

Amy: As a child, I'd attended a Methodist church and sang in the choir, but when I was a teenager, I left. I wasn't happy. I was consumed with trying to be perfect for others.

Colleen: I grew up Catholic, and I remember giving my life to Jesus in second grade, but at the time it didn't do much in my life. I still attend Catholic church with my dad. He has always been an example to me of a godly man.

1. Adapted from the seeJesus network newsletter, Spring 2004, Telford, PA; www.seejesus.net. Used with permission.

Q. Why did you come to the study?

Amy: I was at the end of my rope. I remember saying to myself while standing in the garage, "I'm going to walk out of here." Deep down, I was also searching for something bigger than me. I felt a big void inside. I wanted to listen to the truth, but I wasn't sure what it was.

Colleen: I was mainly focused on changing my husband. I thought that he might be able to learn from the study how to treat me better. But I also knew I was a mess. My marriage was a mess . . . there was no way out. I was so disappointed in myself. I remember at Easter of 2001, before I'd seen the invitation, just crying and crying. When I got the invitation I was struck by the question, "How do you love when you get no love in return?"

Amy: The same was true for me. My whole life was in the toilet, especially my family. My husband thought I was certifiably crazy. He had no clue to what my problem was. The kids weren't happy. I didn't want to get out of bed in the morning.

Q. Prior to the study, when was the last time you'd read a Bible?

Amy: I guess when I was about twelve in Sunday school.

Colleen: We heard the Bible read on Sundays, but I don't ever remember studying the Bible. We kept the Bible in a drawer in our house. My memory of it was that it was gigantic, but recently when I was at my parents, I found it, and it wasn't that big.

Q. What is your memory of our first class?

Colleen: I was struck how Jesus looked at people, and then I realized that he saw me as well. I came out of there wanting to know more. I really didn't know Jesus, and this made the Bible so alive. The historical background made it come alive. It was like going to see a movie in 3-D color for the first time.

114

Amy: I didn't know what the group would be like, but walking into the church felt so good—like I needed to be there. God had been talking to me every week for the past year on Sunday morning telling me to go to church. But I didn't know where to go. It had been more than twenty years since I'd darkened a church door (except for weddings, funerals). The teaching made Jesus real. You created his image through your questions and words. The stories from your life made Jesus real as well. And I loved the people—we were all so different, but we grew to love one another as the group gelled.

Q. What was it like to be around Christians? [Initially I'd been afraid that I wouldn't get any seekers, but then we had more seekers than churchgoers; so I asked several people to join our group. Three men, all older, responded: Henry, Bill, and Al.]

Colleen: When Henry would pray I felt I was right there with God. He was so deep and holy.

Amy: Yes, his voice was both authoritative and confident. I never experienced being with someone like that before. It was like, "Wow!"

Colleen: The same was true with Bill. When he would look at me sometimes it felt like he was looking into me. There was a reverence in him. Al usually sat behind me. I felt his faith and love for God. I'd not met men like this before, except for my dad. I don't feel that from many people. You could sense God's presence in their lives.

Q. What was new to you? What surprised you?

Amy: It was a slow process, like waking up. In the lesson on how the people demanded that Jesus do a sign for them, I asked you about signs and if you could ask God for them. You told me to not hunt for specific signs but to begin to see how God is in everything. When you said that to me . . . and we'd been in the study for six months by then, I had no idea what you were talking about. But now I see him everywhere and in everything. It is hard to imagine how depressing my life was at that time. It was gray, sad, and without hope. In the beginning it was like seeing a ray of light at the end of a dark tunnel. That light grew gradually brighter. The change in me was not instantaneous. Slowly, I began to see that God is in everything and that he really cares for me.

Colleen: I went through a process of challenging some of the beliefs I'd been brought up with. I discovered that Jesus died for me. I'd lived with so much guilt my whole life. Discovering that Jesus died for me wasn't just words now, I know that my name is written on the palm of his hand. I really feel his love for me.

Q. Week after week as you encountered Jesus, what was it like?

Colleen: I couldn't wait to go each week. I don't think I missed once. As the weeks passed by my main thought was, "Eyes off me and on Jesus—God." The picture of "Self" on the throne instead of God that you used to draw really got to me.

Amy: Wonderful. Awesome. I couldn't wait to go; it gave me a purpose. It was also an opportunity to go out, to be social, and to learn.

Colleen: I came to the class in the beginning thinking that it would change my husband—since he came for the first couple of times. Then I began to slowly see that it was me who needed changing. I began to realize that I couldn't change him. I was the problem. But I was seeing my sin in the presence of Jesus. He was loving me all the time. He was looking at me. So I really began to see my sin, but strangely at the same time I saw less of it because I was freed from guilt. There was so much hope that came into my life. Do you remember that one week when

116

I started crying, and I couldn't stop? I was so moved by the way Jesus was. The tears were rolling down my cheeks. It was the lesson on Jesus' humility. I thought of that coworker who'd been so mean to me, and I realized that I didn't want to go in and greet her. You all stopped and prayed for me. I felt so unworthy.

Q. What was it like to attend church regularly?

Amy: I stayed for the worship and I was hooked. Listening to the pastor preach, his passion, and the singing.

Colleen: After the Sunday school class I couldn't get out of there fast enough. But now I go every Sunday.

Q. What changes have you seen in yourself?

Amy: Hope. I smile now. It is an inner confidence. A journey. I can find God in all things, especially the small things. Before I didn't see any of that; now I had a positive outlook because Jesus loved me—this unforgivable sinner. I'd been so angry with God.

Colleen: The biggest change was realizing that no works could get me on the good side of Jesus; just believing him was all that was needed. I never knew that. I was always focused on just being good.

Amy: Before, I'd wanted to change myself. I really identified with the Samaritan woman. I needed that living water. Being quiet is a big change for me—the inner quietness creates an outer quietness. Instead of exploding at home and that push, push, push for control, I now let go of control. I could let go because I wasn't alone. It was safe to be quiet.

I feel that I can get up every day and talk to Jesus. I lay it all out. I can go through each day with a peace in my heart. I saw it at this last Christmas with my boys. It is just an awesome thing. I love reading my Bible. It has completely changed the way I live. Outwardly life has not changed much, but the inside is all different. My kids see it. They ridicule me for it, but they see it. I see changes in them as well and know the Holy Spirit is at work in our lives.

Joy is the other change. Joy in little things. Joy with other Christians. Colleen and I share the love of God. We're on the same page. I discovered that my "little" sister who lives in Arkansas had been praying for over ten years that God would work in my life.

CHAPTER 10

The Spiritual Midwife: Calling

AS A SPIRITUAL MIDWIFE, you will be watching the Spirit move people toward the place of conversion. This is a season of a person's spiritual life that I have already identified as their pregnancy. Describing it with this term almost always brings smiles of recognition when I am teaching a group of Christians about the new birth. We look back at a time of struggle and growing awareness of need, resistance, and perhaps many false starts and then finally surrender, and we see behind all of that the gracious moving of the Holy Spirit leading us to faith in Christ.

The biblical term I have used for this time of spiritual pregnancy is *calling*. Recall our earlier study in 1 Corinthians 1 where Paul described how his listeners received his preaching of the gospel. In their natural state both Jews and Greeks (Gentiles) rejected it, "but to those whom God has *called*, both Jews and Greeks, Christ [is] the power of God and the wisdom of God" (v. 24). When people stayed behind and wanted to hear more about Jesus and then believed in him, Paul understood that they were responding to a call from God. These called ones were then baptized and became the first members of the new church. As I have mentioned, when Paul wrote back to them he frequently reminded them of their calling as the starting point of their Christian life (Rom. 1:6–7; 8:30; 1 Cor. 1:9; Gal. 1:6; 5:8).

The most helpful description I have found of what the Spirit's calling looks like comes from the Westminster Shorter Catechism. Many are familiar with the first question of the catechism that asks, "What is the chief end of man?" and then answers, "Man's chief end is to glorify God and to enjoy him forever." The catechism goes on, through questions and answers, to present the nature of God, the Holy Trinity, the work of God the Father as planner and Creator, the person and work of God the Son as our Redeemer, and finally the work of God the Holy Spirit as he applies to our hearts what Christ accomplished in his death and resurrection. In question 30 the catechism asks, "How does the Spirit apply to us the redemption purchased by Christ?" and answers, "The Spirit applies to us the redemption purchased by Christ by working faith in us and thereby uniting us to Christ in our *effectual calling*." That leads to question 31, "What is effectual calling?"

> Effectual calling is the work of God's Spirit whereby:
>> Convincing us of our sin and misery,
>> Enlightening our minds in the knowledge of Christ, and
>> Renewing our wills,
>> He persuades and enables us to embrace Jesus Christ freely
> offered to us in the gospel.

Carefully reread that answer because it will provide the outline of how I will explain what calling looks like. Note that it is a "*work*" of God's Spirit. In the language of the catechism, that indicates a *process* during which the three activities mentioned go on, until he both persuades and enables us to embrace Jesus Christ. Here is a beautiful way to describe the mystery of the Spirit's work in salvation by grace. He does the work, but in the end we are the ones who respond to the gospel and by faith give ourselves to Jesus. But it is a faith that God has given us ("For it is by grace you have been saved, through faith—and this not from yourselves, it is the gift of God—not by works, so that no one can boast," Eph. 2:8–9). I believe that statement of the catechism is the most helpful brief description of true conversion that I know of: *we embrace Jesus Christ freely offered to us in the gospel.*

CONVINCING US OF OUR SIN AND MISERY

One of the specific purposes of the coming of the Spirit was to convict of sin (John 16:8–11). Anyone who has experienced the new birth has some experience of the inner conviction of his or her growing sense of unworthiness as he or she stands before God. But it is important that we not assume that *our* experience of conviction will be what someone else experiences. I remember hearing the story of a man who had become deeply convicted of his addiction to smoking, and that was what God used to eventually bring him to a place of surrender to Christ. He then spent the rest of his life trying to evangelize by preaching against the evils of tobacco. That may be an extreme example, but the lesson it teaches is important. It will be surprising, as you learn to listen to people, to discover the remarkable and unexpected ways that the Spirit breaks into people's lives.

Frequently this aspect of the work of the Spirit comes before the others. In many cases it is a brokenness that comes about through people's selfish or destructive behavior that makes them long for something better. Often it may mean they are more convinced of their misery than of their sin, but even that can be from the hand of a loving God. I have had people express thanksgiving for an illness or divorce or imprisonment, not because they were good things in themselves, but because it was through these trials that they began to be more open to the things of God.

Misery, however, is not necessarily a prerequisite for faith, and there are others whose conviction of sin is much more in the sense of a spiritual void than of consciousness of overt sin. God feels distant, and they know it, but they don't know how to get to God. Yet for the first time there is actually a desire to find God, and that is something new or it comes with an intensity they have not experienced before. In fact, that is a conviction of the ultimate sin—unbelief. Most people aren't able to express it in those terms and don't even think of unbelief in terms of sin. That was my experience as a teenager from a non-churched family who had never given much thought to God one way or another. I was attending a church because it was expected of me in order to play for their basketball team. But I was oblivious to anything of spiritual value, and whatever I was hearing in church went right over my head. However, that all changed one Sunday when the speaker said, "In everyone's heart there is a spiritual vacuum, and the only one who can fill that vacuum is Jesus Christ." That statement was like an arrow direct to my heart, and from that moment until my conversion I had a continual sense of my need and of God drawing me to himself. But what I was convicted of was my emptiness, not my actions.

I have since discovered that my initial reaction to the convicting work of the Spirit is typical of many. Rather than actually seeking God, I decided that I needed to clean up my act and become more presentable to God. So I set out on a path of moral reformation. Of course, I had no way to know what sin actually was, and I wasn't a particularly bad boy, but I determined that God would be happier with me if I used better language and stopped using God's name in vain. I tried. I was shocked to discover that I couldn't just change my habits simply because I wanted to change. Instead of feeling better about how God must view me, my sense of conviction grew. This is one example of the Spirit using the truth of God's law to convict of sin. In my case, it was the third commandment ("You shall not take the name of the LORD your God in vain," NKJV), even though I wouldn't have expressed it that way at the time. Compared to the deep waters and levels of despair that others have passed through to make themselves acceptable to God, my experience seems trivial. (Read Romans 7:7–12, and notice that God spoke to Paul through the Tenth Commandment, "You shall not covet.") But that is the point—the Spirit worked in me in a way that reached my heart but that might have no impact for someone else.

The Spirit "convinces us of our sin and misery" in an infinite variety of ways. So let me encourage you not to impose a particular pattern on others. It is proper and necessary to speak of sin and its consequences. But repentance, the turning from our sin (and the misery that comes with it), is a process, and a genuinely meaningful understanding of what sin really is only comes *after* we come to Christ. That is when we begin to view sin from God's perspective and realize that our behavior is really only the tip of the iceberg. So while repentance is a vital aspect of conversion, the greater times of repentance will come later.

The Spirit convicts us of our need at a level that will humble us and point us to the sufficiency of Christ.

ENLIGHTENING OUR MINDS IN THE KNOWLEDGE OF CHRIST

Jesus defined eternal life this way: "that they may *know* you, the only true God, and Jesus Christ, whom you have sent" (John 17:3). People often describe their conversion as "coming to *know* Jesus as my Lord and Savior." That is a biblical expression. The kind of knowing described is a relational kind of knowing, not simply knowing information. Through the working of the Holy Spirit, we are actually brought into a relationship of knowing God in Jesus Christ. And like any vital relationship, knowing Christ is a process that will continue into eternity. In fact, the idea of *eternal life* has more to do with the quality of life—that we now know God—than with its length. Consider the apostle Paul, a man who certainly knew Christ. Yet near the end of his ministry he declared that his one great ambition was "to know Christ" (Phil. 3:7–10). That was what he prayed for each of the churches he wrote to during that time (see Eph. 1:15–19; Phil. 1:9–11; Col. 1:9–10). When the Spirit works, "enlightening our minds in the knowledge of Christ," he is beginning a work that will grow into eternity, long after our sin and misery are behind us.

It is a profound thing to be in conversation with people who are beginning to awaken to Jesus and who he is. For many who have been skeptical, things will need to be unlearned, and there will be times of doubt and struggle; for others, in whom there is no knowledge at all, there will need to be a season of teaching;

for still others, who may have been raised in homes and churches where there was good scriptural teaching, the Holy Spirit shines his light on what is already there.

We assume that this process will always take a good deal of time, whatever form the enlightening work of the Spirit may take. But this is not necessarily the case. Consider the example of the jailer who asked Paul and Silas what he needed to do to be saved. He was probably only thinking of staying alive. But Paul told him simply, "Believe in the Lord Jesus, and you will be saved—you and your household." That evening Paul and Silas explained enough that the man and his family believed in Jesus and were baptized (Acts 16:25–34). Does that mean that one visit with a presentation of the "simple gospel" is all that is needed? Not necessarily. But it does mean that it *can* happen. The jailer and his family were ready to believe in Jesus in one evening. That would also mean theirs was a very elementary faith and they would need a great deal of further enlightenment after their conversion.

I encourage those of you who are trained to give concise presentations of the gospel, whether through visitation evangelism or other means, to take enough time to discover where people are in their understanding of Christ. I have been part of gospel presentations (and have done them myself) that would get high marks as sales presentations but were not very sensitive to what people were actually comprehending. If we are part of God's moving in a person's spirit, that is certainly worth a second visit—or a third. I frankly struggle with more scripted approaches to the gospel, but when a person is at the place of believing, that can be exactly what is needed. There are many wonderful examples of people being converted after a presentation of the gospel through a booklet or brief conversation or watching a television program, but that is usually just a small part of their story. I also know of many others who were turned away because of a high-pressure presentation. The key, then, is to seek to know where people are as you meet with them.

It is an interesting question as to how much knowledge of Christ is necessary in order for someone to exercise true saving faith. I don't think it is very much. I often ask people to try to recall how much of the gospel they understood when they first believed. That question is usually answered with smiles and the statement "very little." I am not suggesting that we look for a minimum standard of knowledge, but it is simply a reality in the experience of most people that their awakening to Jesus is usually in very beginning stages when they come to put their faith in him. Just like the greater awareness of our sinfulness, our true knowledge of Christ will grow through our Christian life.

The work of the Spirit draws us *to the person of Christ*. That is one way to sense if a person is being called by the Spirit or is just on a religious quest. Furthermore, people also wrestle with the meaning of the cross and the idea that Jesus died for our sins. Don't expect this to be very well thought through. Keep in mind that the book of Romans was written to explain the work of Christ to those who had *already* believed in him. But it is at the cross that the two works of the Spirit—convincing us of our sin and enlightening our minds in the knowledge of Christ—come together. This means that, however imperfectly, people being called by the Spirit begin to understand that the forgiveness of sin they seek is a result of what Christ did on the cross.

In my experience the most elementary level of knowledge seems to boil down to three things: (1) People have come to a point of realizing they have a need that they cannot meet by themselves. (2) They are aware that in some way Jesus is God and because of this is able to meet that need, and that somehow this is tied into his work on the cross. (3) There is a desire to surrender to Jesus and become his follower. I am not suggesting that this is all we should teach people or that in the experience of many there isn't a far greater level of understanding before conversion. But do not be surprised when you meet people who are alive in Christ, whose faith seems to be genuine, but whose knowledge is very elementary and, in many cases, mixed with error.

This points, obviously, to the need to keep teaching about Christ in our churches and other ministries. Crossing through a phase of growth we call conversion doesn't change the need to learn about Christ and hear the gospel. It is unfortunate that in the understanding of many, presenting the gospel has come to be limited to a few points of explanation about how someone can give their hearts to Christ. The gospel is the story of Jesus and all that he is and has done, and it should always be the core of our teaching. The Spirit will use the gospel to continue to enlighten us so that we grow in the knowledge of Christ.

RENEWING OUR WILLS

We can be totally convinced of our sinful and miserable condition, and we can understand perfectly that Christ's shed blood will cover that sin, but until we *want* Christ, our standing before God will remain unchanged. At one point in his ministry Jesus confronted the scholarly Pharisees and scribes with these words: "You diligently study the Scriptures because you think that by them you possess eternal life. These are the Scriptures that testify about me, yet you refuse to come to me to have life" (John 5:39–40). They had the knowledge, but when the witness of Scripture pointed them to Christ, they refused to come to him. This would be true of all of us apart from the work of the Holy Spirit.

The good news is that the Spirit *does* change our desires. In the words of the Westminster Shorter Catechism, the Spirit persuades as well as enables us to embrace Jesus Christ. Consider this description from Paul's letter to Titus:

> At one time we too were foolish, disobedient, deceived and enslaved by all kinds of passions and pleasures. We lived in malice and envy, being hated and hating one another. But when the kindness and love of God our Savior appeared, he saved us, not because of righteous things we had done, but because of his mercy. He saved us through the washing of rebirth and renewal by the Holy Spirit, whom he poured out on us generously through Jesus Christ our Savior. (Titus 3:3–6)

Keep in mind again that this renewal of the will is part of the *process* of calling. In many cases the movement of a person's desire will be from a place of indifference to one of resistance and even outright hatred rather than willingness. The fact that someone is actively resisting God may be an indicator that he or she is no longer spiritually dead. Often people will do and say very unacceptable things as they fight against the call of the Spirit. They may be closer to the kingdom than you think.

When Jesus called Paul, he asked him if it was hard for him to "kick against the goads" (Acts 26:14). This was an allusion to a sharp prod that a farmer would hold in front of him to keep his ox or donkey from kicking him. Paul's persecution of the believers was an expression of his fighting against Jesus who was in control all along. That is certainly not how those early

Christians saw it. But when actually confronted by Jesus, who called his name, Paul surrendered very quickly.

You will discover that people's interest in the gospel will grow strong and then will die away. People may appear willing, but it could be more a desire to be polite than real spiritual interest. This is especially the case when talking with someone from a culture that places more value on saving face than on honest response. Only God knows what is going on in the heart. In the parable of the sower Jesus spoke of the seed of the gospel falling on all different kinds of soil, with only the prepared soil actually yielding fruit (Matt. 13:1–9, 18–23). You and I are to try to faithfully speak and live the gospel and pray that the Spirit will be at work in the heart.

We need to be cautious about using human persuasion to push for a decision for Jesus. There are certainly times when the Spirit presses upon a person the urgency of believing in Jesus, and he can use a human vehicle to do that. Very often that comes as people sit under the preaching of the Word of God. But as we work with people individually or in small groups, I believe our role should be that of gentle encouragement, not pressing to close the deal. Remember, we are midwives, not salesmen, and a wise midwife knows that the baby will come when the baby is ready.

During a presentation to a Prison Fellowship group I was discussing this topic of people's willingness to believe. A prisoner named Jim asked to speak. He told briefly about his own conversion, which he understood with greater clarity because of the birthline discussion. But then he described his following the course of many zealous new converts and trying to convince everyone in his cellblock to become a follower of Christ. Finally after a great deal of arm-twisting he convinced his friend Bob to pray a prayer to be saved. Bob prayed the prayer but then would have nothing more to do with Jim. Later an older Christian explained to Jim what had happened: "Jim, the difference is that *Jesus* converted you, but *you* converted your friend." I have always remembered that as a good explanation of the difference between human persuasion and the Spirit's renewing our wills.

Thankfully the story doesn't end there. After Jim told his story, I began using it as an illustration each time I would teach another group of prisoners. Imagine my surprise and delight when, about a year later, I was interrupted while telling that story by a hand going up. "I'm Bob!" It took more time than Jim had wanted, but Bob did come to believe, and the Lord even used Jim's misguided but sincere witness as a key part of his work in Bob. God is greater than our mistakes and misstatements.

The outline provided by the Westminster Shorter Catechism only gives a starting point. These are not three firm categories, and even if they were, there is no fixed order in which they are experienced. Often, like Cornelius, people are ready and willing and are waiting to hear of Jesus. Missionaries tell stories of visiting remote tribes and villages of people who had been told to wait for someone who would tell them about a Savior. Other times people know a great deal about Jesus but need the Spirit to bring home the reality of what it means to be a sinner. I have heard this from many people raised in Christian homes. Then there are stories, particularly by converts from Islam or people bound up by addictions, of visions and dreams of Jesus. People have told me about other dramatic experiences that can't be explained (nor should we try) but were definite steps toward eventual conversion. And the Spirit can also call in a quiet and gentle voice, and people respond simply and without much upheaval.

This is what Jesus was speaking about when he described the mysterious blowing of the wind: "The wind blows wherever it pleases. . . . So it is with everyone born of the Spirit" (John 3:8). We are in the presence of divine mystery when we talk about the work of God in the soul.

> I know not why God's wondrous grace to me he has made
> known,
> Nor why, unworthy, Christ in love redeemed me for his own.
>
> I know not how this saving faith to me he did impart,
> Nor how believing in his Word wrought peace within my
> heart.
>
> I know not how the Spirit moves, convincing men of sin,
> Revealing Jesus through the Word, creating faith in him.
>
> But "I know whom I have believed, and am persuaded that
> he is able
> To keep that which I've committed unto him against that day."
>
> —DANIEL W. WHITTLE, 1883, BASED ON 2 TIMOTHY 1:12

CHAPTER 11

The Spiritual Midwife: Conversion

IT IS NOW TIME to look more closely at the actual experience of conversion. The importance of a personal, conscious commitment to Christ is one of the marks of an evangelical, at least as the word is used in the United States, and that is clearly supported by the biblical teaching we have examined. However, in a great deal of our evangelical culture it is assumed that people will have a very *specific* point in their spiritual journey that marks their conversion. Teaching about the Christian life or training in evangelism starts at that point and goes on from there. It is important to examine that assumption more carefully.

Dr. Richard Peace of Fuller Theological Seminary has written a book with the title *Conversion in the New Testament—Paul and the Twelve*. The book begins with a careful analysis of what many people consider to be the basic model of conversion—that of the apostle Paul. But then Dr. Peace writes about the conversion of the twelve original apostles and raises the intriguing question of *when* those first disciples were converted. They *were* converted—that is certain—but *when* doesn't seem to be an issue. In my own classroom and seminar teaching about conversion, I now begin by passing along Dr. Peace's question about the conversion of the Twelve. I have found it to be a great discussion starter in the evangelical church of our time, whether in the United States or overseas.

This is not just a question of understanding our own experiences as we come to Christ. I agree with the conclusion of Dr. Peace as he relates the two different models of conversion to the evangelistic practice of the church. He says, "My core perspective in all this is quite simple. I have come to believe that *how we conceive of conversion determines how we do evangelism.* The equation is really that straightforward."[1] I would add my own conviction that how we conceive of conversion determines how we undertake the *discipleship* of those who confess to be followers of Christ.

Not long ago I was presenting this material to a group of pastors involved in urban ministry in various communities of Philadelphia. One of the men stopped me and made this insightful comment: "It just occurred to me that we have meetings wrestling with why our evangelistic follow-up isn't more effective, but now I wonder if the problem is not follow-up, but how well we understand what it means to be converted. It seems to me that if people's conversion came about through the work of the Holy Spirit, they would *want* to grow and we wouldn't have to chase after them."

1. Richard V. Peace, *Conversion in the New Testament: Paul and the Twelve* (Grand Rapids, MI: Wm. B. Eerdmans, 1999), 286.

WHAT IS CONVERSION?

In this book I have been using *conversion* to describe that time in an individual's spiritual journey when he or she consciously comes to trust in Christ as Lord and Savior. This is the X on the birthline. Conversion is the human response to the call of the Holy Spirit. Because we are now spiritually alive, "begotten from above," we can hear the message and *embrace Jesus Christ freely offered to us in the gospel.*

PHYSICAL AND SPIRITUAL BIRTH

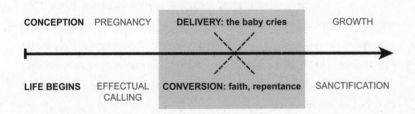

Physical birth

| CONCEPTION | PREGNANCY | DELIVERY: the baby cries | GROWTH |

| LIFE BEGINS | EFFECTUAL CALLING | CONVERSION: faith, repentance | SANCTIFICATION |

Spiritual birth—*regeneration*

In teaching this to a group, I describe conversion by talking about the *delivery* of the baby. Typically when the baby is actually delivered, he or she announces it with a hearty scream. I always get smiles as I describe this because it is such a part of all of our lives. But after I give a good yell in imitating the cry of the new baby, I ask the group, "And what do we say? Johnny's alive? But Johnny's *been alive*—that's not new. *But now it's time for Johnny to go public!*" Once my audience sees that, I add, "And that is what happens with conversion. We have been alive—something within us has been drawing us to Jesus. We think about him in ways we didn't before; we see our hopeless standing before God and know we need to trust in Jesus. And finally we can't keep it in any longer, and we *go public* in one way or another. We cry out to Jesus, and we let it be known that we now desire to follow him. We know that in physical birth pregnancy takes more or less nine months. How long does our spiritual pregnancy take? Nine months? Possibly. Nine years? Possibly. Nine days? Very possibly!" This is when I make the point that just how, and how long, it has taken God to bring us to the place of conversion will be different for every person.

The essential idea of conversion is *turning*. There is turning *from* our sin, which is another way of defining repentance, and turning *to* Christ, which is another way of defining faith. To put it another way, repentance and faith are the two sides of the one coin—conversion. The end result of conversion is that we are embracing Jesus, who is offered to us in the gospel. But we embrace Jesus because we have given up the embrace of our sin. Of course, both our repentance and faith are very immature, but they still represent a real turning point in our lives.

To explain how conversion is experienced I literally walk from one end of a room to the other (or the platform if I am preaching). On one wall I picture my selfish, sinful ways. On the opposite wall, I picture Christ as Lord and Savior who died for my sin. The point is that I can't focus on Christ unless I turn away from my sin. This is repentance and faith, and they must go together.

To demonstrate this I first walk straight toward the wall picturing my sin, and as I walk I describe my hearing of the gospel and my finally deciding to *turn*—which I do with a very sharp turn. Then I begin to walk in the opposite direction, toward the wall picturing Christ. "What have I demonstrated?" I ask, and people immediately respond, "That is conversion." Then I do the same walk a second time, but in this instance I make my turning in a wide arc (depending on how big the room is). As I walk, I slowly describe my life as a dawning awareness of need and awakening to Christ. By the end of my walk I am facing in the opposite direction of how I started, looking now at the wall that represents Christ. Again I ask the question, "What have I just demonstrated?" and while people are slower to respond, eventually they agree that I have just demonstrated conversion. The point is that I *have* turned, not *when* I turned. I then apply this by asking people to consider the direction of their lives, not whether or not they have had an experience they would identify as a conversion. The issue is what direction we are walking in: Are we living for ourselves, whether that means moral or immoral living, or do we trust in Christ and desire to follow him?

THE EXPERIENCE OF CONVERSION

Frequently I ask the members of a group I am teaching to describe their conversion in terms of the birthline. I have had some students erase the X and replace it with a parenthesis. They say they can remember when they weren't believers and then when they were, but they can't be sure when they actually crossed over. Other times students have added several more X marks. They think of their conversion as a series of decisions and can't be certain which time they prayed to receive Christ was the "real" prayer, or possibly each decision was another step in their conversion.

You may recall that it was my experience of hearing more and more of these stories that caused me to change the way I drew the X on the birthline. I hope that at this stage of our studies, including rethinking your own conversion experience, you too are comfortable with the variety of ways people actually pass through this stage of conversion. In fact, for most people their conversion is something they don't begin to understand until some time after they have gone through it.

While I was staying in Spain I had a conversation with a man originally from Lebanon who owned a shop I visited often. He had identified himself to me as a member of the Orthodox church but also was quite emphatic in calling himself a "believer." When we had an opportunity for a quiet conversation, I told him about my work on the book and asked him to give me more detail about his own spiritual journey, which he was happy to do. He talked about his family history and the terrible persecution that Christians of the Middle East had faced for centuries. When I asked, he told me that "born again" was not a phrase that he heard growing up, although he knew of the passage in John 3. As we moved on to talk about his personal pilgrimage, it became evident to me that there had been a work of the Spirit giving him a deep personal trust in Christ. Even though they were not couched in evangelical terminology, I was very moved by his expressions of faith and repentance. Toward the end of our conversation he said, "You can be sure that there are many sincere believers in Jesus in the Middle East who are paying a price for their faith."

This conversion story is a reminder that multitudes of people in churches do not think of conversion in the way that most of us have been taught. This is not to presume that all members of these churches are "saved," any more than we should presume this about those in our evangelical churches who know how to use a more familiar terminology. Only God sees the heart, and we need to be cautious in how we judge others.

I am not trying to minimize the importance of conversion. It is not only taught in Scripture, but it is something we need as human beings. That is why I use the image of the newborn baby crying out. The cry of faith is something *we* need to hear as well as God. There is an interesting statement in Romans 10 that speaks to the importance of a confession of faith. "If you confess with your mouth, 'Jesus is Lord,' and believe in your heart that God raised him from the dead, you will be saved. For it is with your heart that you believe and are justified, and it is with your mouth that you confess and are saved . . . for, 'Everyone who calls on the name of the Lord will be saved'" (vv. 9–10, 13).

Even if an inward conversion may not be a clear moment for some, it still needs to be defined by some form of public confession of Jesus. In the early church, as well as for newly evangelized people today, that was marked by baptism. In cultures where baptism is commonplace there also needs to be some other form of public statement. I believe this is true as well for those baptized as infants. In our church we ask prospective members to make a statement of faith to our elders. That is often introduced by a personal story of how they came to faith, but it always needs to include a confession of Jesus Christ as Lord and Savior. Those of you who see people coming to faith outside of a church context should provide some way of allowing a public confession. Of course, the best way is to point them to a good church that they can join, but if that is impossible you need to find some other way.[2]

2. In my book, *The Walk*, I entitle the second chapter, "Do I Have to Go to Church?" and answer emphatically, YES. "Being a disciple of Jesus is a personal response to the call of Jesus, but we are also called to become a part of a community,

It is important to note that I am talking about verbalizing a confession of Christ as Lord. This is not the same as giving a testimony. It is the practice in some settings to ask a new convert to immediately begin telling the story of his or her conversion. There may be situations when this is appropriate, but far too often the tendency is to give special attention to the more sensational aspects of the conversion. In the end, too much emphasis is placed on the experience itself. If we elevate an experience, we may be giving a person false assurance. A true conversion will show itself in a new heart and new thoughts and new directions. We need to give the new baby time to grow.

A CASE STUDY: DOUG LOGAN

I was born in Patterson, New Jersey, to Douglas and Hattie Logan. I was their youngest child and only son, a brother to five older sisters. The structural dynamics of my household were unbalanced: my mother was a God-fearing Christian woman and my father was an abusive alcoholic. I was raised in the black Baptist church, as most African Americans were at the time, and "being Christian" was an assumed part of the culture. While I am grateful for my religious upbringing, it did cause me to have a distorted view of Christianity and Jesus. I did not have an understanding of the gospel message, and Jesus was nothing more than someone who you go to in crisis.

When I was twelve years old, my mother died on New Year's Day. I was a mama's boy, and I felt totally alone in the world. My

---

a fellowship, of disciples" (*The Walk: Steps for New and Renewed Followers of Jesus* [Phillipsburg, NJ: P&R, 2009], 36.). The virtual impossibility of growing as a disciple of Jesus without community is not a sign of weakness on our parts, it is simply the nature of how God has designed for us to grow and reproduce.

father would either be drunk or gone for days on end. At this point I began to hang on the streets doing things I ought not, but for the most part I was considered a pretty good kid. After some time I moved in with my sister, who later moved us to North Carolina. I started college at North Carolina A&T State University studying political science, following the footsteps of my hero, Rev. Jesse Jackson. After two years of school, the money that my mother had left me for college was depleted and I was unable to finish. So I moved back to New Jersey and opened a barbershop. As a barber I met a number of people, namely my wife, and a number of Christian men who were to become instrumental in my salvation. Since I attended church regularly I still had a moral values system, but I did not know Jesus. If someone ever asked me about being a Christian, I would respond that I attended Christ Baptist Church, and this answer usually sufficed.

Thankfully, there were a few people who directly asked me whether my life was totally given over to Jesus or not, and one of them was named Jay Sykes. Jay had met Jesus in a very real way three years earlier, and he would not accept my record of church attendance as an answer to his questions regarding my soul. He watched me continuously live in unrepentant sin, and he was not afraid to confront me with the fact that I was going to hell. Because of his persistent confrontation, coupled with the conviction I felt, I radically met the Lord one night at 2 am. In the middle of the night the Spirit of God confronted me and I yielded to his will and received Jesus Christ as Savior and Lord. As said before, I had attended church all my life, but things were different now. In the past I had had emotional experiences that had given me a "spiritual high" that resulted in empty promises to God or brief periods of good works. But before long I was always back to my old ways, living in unrepentant sin. Showing up at church usually made me feel like I was cleaning my slate, and that God and I were on pretty good terms. But little did I know that my life prior to Christ reflected nothing of true Christianity. In fact, soon after my conversion I noticed that I no longer felt "OK" with my periods of sinning. I was grieved about my sin and I genuinely desired to live for Christ. Church was no longer a place for me to clean myself up, but rather, it was a place I could go to fellowship with other Christians and freely worship God because I knew that because of Christ *I was clean*. Because of the Holy Spirit's work in my life I now really understood the gospel and it began to inform every area of my life. I had been transformed, and those around me recognized that I was not the person they knew before. Immediately after my conversion, along with a minister from my church I began to serve homeless people on the streets of Philadelphia. This minister discipled me and, within six years, I was licensed and ordained to the gospel ministry, and was subsequently called to my first church in 2003.

CHAPTER 12

The Spiritual Midwife: First Steps of Faith

SHORTLY BEFORE I LEFT to write this book, I spent an afternoon with Don and Jane (not their real names), a couple who have lived and ministered for years in an Islamic country that is hostile to any gospel witness. I wanted to ask whether the birthline was a helpful idea in terms of their ministry experience. They responded that it was very helpful in illustrating how the conversions they have witnessed came about. Not only was the concept of process true to their experience, but they also were helped by not having to think of conversion as a specific moment. "We don't pay as much attention to statements about conversion as we do to signs of a changed life," they told me. "We watch to see how the believers treat others and for a spirit of humility—these are more important than a conversion experience to us."

Jane told the story of Chadra (not her real name), a woman who came to their home to do housework and cooking. Jane said that her coming to faith took about ten years. Chadra listened in as the family worshiped together, then gradually paid more and more attention until finally she felt comfortable sitting with the family, although she never said anything about her faith. Because other believers would come from time to time to the home, Chadra watched how they treated one another and was very struck by the contrast with her culture. Finally she listened in as a Muslim-background believer told his story to a group. Later she told Jane that she knew it was all true and that now she was a person "on the way." Unfortunately the word *Christian* has a very negative connotation in that country, and it is seldom used for sincere followers of Christ. Jane said that the idea of being "in the way of Jesus" seems to be a natural expression for those who come to faith in this setting.

Jane also told me about another woman, Fatima (not her real name), who took about six years to come to faith. She was an upper-class, educated woman and visited with Jane socially. They would frequently discuss matters of faith. But it was through two dreams, which Fatima described to Jane, that she came to confess Christ. The first one was about a man who told her about her life and her need for Christ. She spent the night crying over her sins. In the second dream she saw Jane pointing her to what she knew to be the tree of life. She subsequently suffered terrible persecution but never regretted her choice to follow Christ.

THOSE WHO ARE BORN WILL GROW

When a child is delivered into the light of day, we expect that child to continue to grow. I used the word *continue* deliberately—it is the next step in the process. The child has been growing for nine months, but now that growth will look somewhat different. Each baby grows at its own pace, much of that having to do with the circumstances of the baby's birth. Some are sickly at birth and even addicted to substances from their mother. Babies who have received good prenatal care usually grow much more quickly, at least at first. In time the baby crawls and then takes those first shaky steps. These are all things that are part of our common experience with children. Of course, there are examples of babies who die, and sadly many die through abortions before they ever take a first breath on their own, but we are using what ordinarily happens to give us a picture of the spiritual life. We should not try to make a parallel of every detail. At this stage we are more like nurses or parents than midwives, but the imagery is still helpful.

The teaching of Scripture is that a genuine conversion will be followed by growth in Christ (recall the study of 1 Thessalonians 1). It is not just that those who are in Christ *ought* to grow (which of course is true), but *where there is spiritual birth there will be growth*—it is a normal part of the process. On the birthline diagram this phase of our spiritual life is labeled *sanctification*, and it is as much a work of the Spirit as all the other aspects of God's work of salvation. Almost without exception when the apostle Paul calls for a change in attitude or behavior, he appeals to the fact that they *have been* changed. "Do not offer the parts of your body to sin, as instruments of wickedness, but rather offer yourselves to God, as *those who have been brought from death to life*" (Rom. 6:13). What is already true on the inside, because of the new birth, needs to work its way out into daily conduct and relationships. Taking off the "old self" and putting on the "new self" assumes that we are raised with Christ, and our life is "*now* hidden with Christ in God" (Col. 3:1–4:1).

PHYSICAL AND SPIRITUAL BIRTH

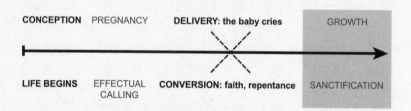

Physical birth

| CONCEPTION | PREGNANCY | DELIVERY: the baby cries | GROWTH |

| LIFE BEGINS | EFFECTUAL CALLING | CONVERSION: faith, repentance | SANCTIFICATION |

Spiritual birth—*regeneration*

When we nurture the new believer with this assumption, it means we can expect receptivity to teaching and direction. We feed a newborn baby, but the hunger comes from within. If your new "convert" shows little interest in joining with others in the worship of God or in studying Scripture, perhaps you need to go more slowly in your work and not think of him or her as converted. Growth comes from within, and while there are certainly things we can do to encourage it, we can't make it happen. Unfortunately, there are so many superficial "decisions for Jesus" where there is no interest in growth that a category has been created called "carnal Christian." It is to be expected, states this teaching, that a person believes in Jesus but may not want to follow him. Another way this is expressed is to say that we can accept Jesus as *Savior* but not as *Lord*, as though there are normally two stages of conversion. There are certainly examples of people who profess Christ but are not genuinely converted, and other times when it takes a while for the new life to become evident. It is not always easy to distinguish the two. But Scripture is clear: someone who is alive in Christ *will grow*, and it is our privilege and responsibility to feed and nurture that new life.

GROWING UP ISN'T EASY

We need to be prepared for the fact that newborns can be messy. In terms of spiritual nurture that means we will find ourselves dealing with issues that don't seem to fit into the categories most of us are comfortable with. In the moral climate of our postmodern culture, we need to recognize that not only are people starting a new walk with Christ, but their whole conscience and character may need to be reformed. This will take time, and we need to be discerning about what needs to come first.

The key, once again, is patience and learning to listen. We are eager to pass along all our knowledge and spiritual lessons, but that may not be what a person is ready for. As in the case of conversion, try to recall the process you went through in your early days as a believer. Your experience will not necessarily be the same, but in all likelihood you had many ups and downs and times of confusion and doubt. Be patient and answer the questions people are asking, even as you encourage them to take further steps of faith.

I have observed a pattern of spiritual development in which the Lord seems to put some people who have serious addictions, psychological afflictions, broken relationships, etc., into a sort of spiritual incubator. For a time they seem totally free of whatever has troubled them, and they grow in their relationship to Christ unhindered by the past. In some cases that is a permanent deliverance. But for most there comes a time, possibly even years later, when they need to face this curse from their old life and conquer it in the power of that same Holy Spirit who brought them to faith. This is never easy, but as they face the issue in the light of their relationship to Christ and with the help of you or other believers, it usually marks a significant step in their spiritual growth. Don't be surprised, however, if there seems to be a turning back or a time of decline as they fight the battle. We may not see Christ triumph before they pass out of our lives, but if God has begun the work he will complete it (Phil. 1:6).

THE EXPERIENCE OF MARY

I remember a young woman who made an appointment to see me after visiting our church one Sunday. As she told her story, it was clear that she was a deeply troubled person with real doubts about her relationship with Christ. She had just returned from a program of studying abroad and during that time had essentially abandoned any pretense of Christian morality. Before I tried to offer any judgment of her situation, I asked her to trace out for me her spiritual pilgrimage. With my questions guiding her, she told about growing up in an unchurched family and then first hearing of Christ through the ministry of Young Life, which had an active club in her high school. She described the change of heart as she felt drawn to Christ and then the commitment she had made to him during one of the camps. She had become active in the Young Life group for believers but had never gotten active in a church. She then went on to tell more about the life that followed.

As I listened to her story, I asked Mary why she had come to church and then had come to talk to me. She wasn't sure what I was getting at. So I said, "Mary, it seems to me that you have described a change in your heart that you can't escape. You probably know others who have made a similar commitment but have just walked away. *You* can't do that, can you? I know you are ashamed of your behavior, but why are you ashamed? It isn't just moral failure you are ashamed of—it's that you know you have dishonored Christ, and that breaks your heart. That tells me that the Christ who saved you will not let you go." As I spoke, there were tears in Mary's eyes, and when I finished, she spontaneously fell on her knees and prayed a prayer of heartfelt repentance.

The approach I used with Mary is similar to the way I approach many people I talk to about their struggles. By tracing out their birthline, I gain a sense of whether or not I am talking to someone who has been called by the Spirit and was truly converted. If I become convinced that the Spirit has worked in calling them to Christ (and of course we can never know that with absolute certainty), then I go back and build on that foundation. In Mary's case, I became convinced she was troubled because of the convicting work of the Holy Spirit. Appealing to that fact worked far more powerfully than just talking about her behavior. In the end, she repented because she had a clearer picture of God's grace toward her.

Sadly, we often learn more about God's love through our failures than through our successes. I see that to be like the baby's first steps in which the excited parents are sitting and watching as those first shaky steps are taken. And what inevitably happens? The baby falls—a failure! And do parents scold the baby? Of course not! They pick the baby up, give her a big hug, and let her try again when she is ready. Is God our Father angry when we venture out but then fail in our attempts to be obedient Christians? I think he is more like the proud parents who are so pleased at the attempt to walk that the "failure" is hardly noticed. This is not to excuse willful disobedience but is merely an observation about how to help those who stumble in their efforts to walk away from the old life. I believe that is the kind of environment we want to encourage in our churches and other ministries as we try to help the new believers in their walk with Christ.

WHAT IS DISCIPLESHIP?[1]

The word *discipleship* has come to be used for various programs and methods of training people to grow to a more mature faith in Christ. New approaches are constantly appearing, but those involved in discipleship ministries are also questioning why they are not more effective. Jim Petersen is a vice president of the most widely respected ministry devoted to discipleship, the Navigators. In 1993 Petersen wrote a book published by NavPress called *Lifestyle Discipleship*. The book begins with this startling statement: "Thirty years of discipleship programs and we are not discipled."[2] Petersen was saying that something is flawed about the way discipleship is practiced by the evangeli-

---

1. The next two sections are the basis for *The Walk: Steps for New and Renewed Followers of Jesus.* In that book I use an outline of Romans as a basis for a plan of growth as a disciple. I also dwelt at greater length on the question "What is discipleship?" in a booklet of that title published by P&R Publishing in 2011.

2. Jim Petersen, *Lifestyle Discipleship* (Colorado Springs: NavPress, 1993), 15.

cal church, including his own organization. To their credit, it was the Navigators themselves who published the book and welcomed the ideas of one of their key leaders to rethink what discipleship means.

While Petersen writes very helpful things about discipleship, he builds much of his teaching on a basic assumption that I believe to be at the root of many of the problems he is concerned about. "To be competent in discipling others, we need a thorough understanding of the dynamics of the growth process. . . . We will start at the beginning of the spiritual life: at conversion."[3] I completely agree with the first part of the statement, that "we need a thorough understanding of the dynamics of the growth process." That is the purpose of this book. But the beginning of the growth process is *not* conversion, as we have seen.

We need to view discipleship as our part of what the Spirit is doing in people's lives, including the time before conversion. Look again at the important passage called the Great Commission (Matt. 28:18–20). Jesus commanded his disciples to "go and make disciples of all nations." Making disciples was to include two steps: "baptizing them" and "teaching them to obey everything I have commanded you." In other words, in this key passage what we now call evangelism and discipleship are really two stages of *making disciples*. The Great Commission is not to go and make *converts*, particularly if that is understood to be getting decisions for Jesus. The charge is to *make disciples*. The first stage is to bring people to the place where they are ready to publicly profess Christ and identify themselves with his people, and the second stage is to teach them what it means to continue obediently following Christ. But both stages are part of discipleship. *Discipleship is the*

3. Ibid., 69–70.

process of calling people to follow Jesus and then walking with them through that process.

In my own ministry I have been increasingly drawn back to the basic idea of a disciple as one who follows Jesus. In the language of those Muslim converts, we are "in the way of Jesus." In the last chapter I described my simple demonstration of conversion as making either a sharp turn or walking in a wide arc. But at the end of the demonstration I am facing in a direction that means I am following Christ. That is the challenge I prefer to put before people rather than appealing for a decision to "accept Jesus" or words to that effect. This allows for the fact that some people have gone farther down the path away from Christ. At the point of their turning they may be in much worse shape than the moral, churchgoing person who is nevertheless still turned toward self. I can acknowledge that people are in different places in their understanding and actions, but I can still ask everyone I'm speaking to, "As best you know your own heart, are you walking on that path *toward Jesus*? If you are, then come and join us. We need you, and you need us." As the label *Christian* has less and less meaning, I wonder if it wouldn't be better for believers to identify themselves simply as followers of Jesus.

The word that is frequently used by the apostle Paul to describe the new life is *walk*. In the New International Version, the word is usually translated "live," but the literal idea of *walk* captures the picture of following Jesus. We are moving in a new direction (Eph. 2:1–2, 10; 4:17; 5:1–2, 8, 15). They may be faltering steps, but they are toward Christ. Perhaps the best expression of the work of the Spirit putting us on a new path is Galatians 5:25: "Since we *live* by the Spirit, let us *keep in step* with the Spirit."

The call to follow Jesus—our being led to the place of conversion as well as our walk following conversion—is an important reminder that we need to hear the gospel at every phase of our spiritual lives. In his book on conversions in the New Testament, Richard Peace presents the case for reading the Gospel of Mark as a series of invitations to follow Jesus for those who are not yet sure what it means to believe. The opening sentence of Mark—"The beginning of the gospel of Jesus Christ, the Son of God"—makes that point clearly. We need to recommend the reading of Mark as people begin to be interested in Jesus, not just after they have been converted. *This is the gospel.* That does not fit our contemporary reductions of the gospel to a few key points, but it does fit the idea of authentic conversion as a process that leads us to be followers of Jesus.

Many of the first disciples of Jesus were followers first and came to believe as they were following (John 2:11; 6:66–69; 16:31; 20:28–31). So what comes first—the following or the believing? Or is there really a difference? Aren't these different ways to emphasize what it means to be a disciple of Jesus? In nations where there is a veneer of Christianity and believing can be a very superficial affirmation, such as the United States, I'm convinced that the issue of *following Jesus* needs to be heard a great deal more than calls for making some sort of decision or acceptance.

GOSPEL DISCIPLING

The core problem with discipleship, as it is now understood in the evangelical church, is not with *methodology* but with *content*. In one form or another, discipleship is typically the teaching of what a Christian is to believe and how he or she is to live. The emphasis is usually on what are called the Christian disciplines, such as Bible reading and prayer as well as church participation and service to others. Rather than trying to repackage that basic approach, we need to go back and recognize that the essential element of discipleship needs to be *the gospel*. The term I have been using for this is *gospel discipling*. When I use the phrase *go back*, I mean that I believe this was how Paul followed up his converts. He kept teaching the gospel both *before* and *after* men and women came to believe it.

An excellent example of this is the book of Romans. We treat it too often as an abstract theological masterpiece, but it was written by a missionary who led people to faith in Christ and then was constantly working to see that faith grow. Review the introductory verses to his letter (1:1–17). Paul carefully defined the gospel in his first words (vv. 2–4) and wrote that he was coming to "preach the gospel also to you who are at Rome" (v. 15). Who was he writing to? "To all in Rome who are loved by God and *called* to be saints" (v. 7). He had already been inspired by reports of their faith (vv. 8,12). In other words, he was coming to preach the gospel to the *church*, those who already believed it because they had experienced God's call to belong to Jesus Christ. Paul then goes into great detail about the blessings that come to those who are called, particularly justification, sanctification, and adoption (Rom. 3–8), and in view of God's mercy the call to live a life of submission and obedience (Rom. 12–14). We could think of Mark as telling us the *story of the gospel* and Paul in Romans as telling us the *meaning of the story*.[4]

4. These topics are given an expanded explanation in *The Walk*, chapters 4–11, as part of my discussion of discipleship through the gospel.

Therefore, Romans defines preaching the gospel in a context of *discipleship* rather than of evangelism, to use our modern distinction. This gospel "is the power of God for the salvation of everyone who believes" (v. 16). It is important to note that the word "believes" is in the present tense, which is best translated in a progressive sense, "is believing." Therefore, the power of God for salvation is much more than that aspect of salvation that occurs at conversion. As people continue to believe the gospel and gain even more insight into its depth, they will also continue to be empowered by the gospel. This is the *essence* of gospel discipling.

CAN WE BE SURE?

It is when people identify themselves as followers of Jesus that they also grow in an assurance that the new birth is real for them. This is usually called *assurance of salvation*. The apostle Paul talks about the Spirit himself who "testifies with our spirit," assuring us that we are children of God. The context of that phrase is the struggle of the believer to live in the Spirit rather than in the flesh (Rom. 8:12–16).

Allowing time for baby steps in the walk of faith, and for the Spirit to be the one to give assurance of faith, is a distinct contrast to instruction many of us have received in evangelism classes or in training to be a counselor in large crusades. We were taught that immediately upon leading someone to pray "the sinner's prayer" we should extend a hand to them and say, "Welcome to the kingdom of God!" If this is confusing to the person, then we are to review the facts of the gospel presentation and assure them that anyone who prayed as they just did, to receive the gift of eternal life, is a child of God. It is certainly true that God's salvation is a gift, but an essential part of that gift is a changed heart, and a changed heart will be expressed in a changed life—a life of following Jesus. Give that new life a chance to begin to show itself. It is important to allow time for the Spirit to give this assurance to those who are professing to follow Christ.

In recent years I have found that my best counsel to doubters has been to point them to the Communion table rather than to ask them to evaluate the genuineness of their experience or depth of faith. That has been the same source of comfort in my own times of doubting. We come to the Lord's Table and the symbols of his body and blood given for us, and we eat and drink. Effectively we are saying, "Lord, if there is to be any hope for eternal life, I confess again today that I am placing my hope in Jesus alone." And we make that confession before others in a tangible way. It is very important that we help people find Christ as their source of assurance, not their past or present feelings.

CHAPTER 13

How the Children of Christian Families Come to Faith

BEFORE I SAT DOWN to begin writing this chapter, Sandy and I were discussing the situations that some of our children are facing. As we ended our conversation we stopped and prayed together for each of our children and grandchildren, mentioning their names before God and asking his guidance and protection for each one of them.

I mention this incident because it points up a particular issue in any consideration of the new birth—our own children. To the best of my knowledge, my parents never prayed for me, nor did they give much consideration to my religious training. But after my conversion it became very important to me that I have a wife who shared my faith. Our wedding marked the beginning of a Christian home, and I had engraved on the inside of Sandy's wedding ring Psalm 34:3, "O magnify the LORD with me, and let us exalt his name together" (KJV). We prayed for our children before they were born, we prayed with them while they were with us, and we have sought to raise them in a home filled with the love of Christ and love for one another. We have done that *very* imperfectly, but however flawed our home life has been, it is a radically different spiritual environment than what I experienced growing up.

When I use the phrase *our children*, I am referring to children raised in families that are self-consciously Christian. This means more than going to church or saying grace before meals. It means there are consistent efforts to have a Christ-centered home. I don't want to offer a formula for what that looks like because in my experience "successful" Christian homes look so different from one another.

Each one of you reading this will have a different recollection of the spiritual environment of the family you grew up in. Some are in the line of several generations of godly families, whereas others of you have no idea what a Christian home is like in terms of personal experience. But whatever our background is, it is to be expected that as we think about how we can serve as spiritual midwives, our children will receive particular attention. This will be also true in our churches; so I am also thinking of pastors and those of you working in various children's and youth ministries.[1]

Is the new birth different for our children? Do they inherit our faith somehow? Or are they lost pagans whose only advantage is that they will hear the gospel earlier in their lives than most? These are the kinds of questions that go through the minds of Christian parents.

1. See *How Our Children Come to Faith* (Phillipsburg, NJ: P&R Publishing, 2006). This is a booklet covering the ideas in this chapter and designed to be handed out to parents as they present their children for baptism or dedication.

The challenge in seeking biblical answers to these questions is that the New Testament church is what could be called a first-generation church. That means it was a church formed by those who came to faith out of a situation of unbelief, whether they were Jews or Gentiles. These were people who heard the gospel as something brand-new, and as the Spirit called them to Christ, they were converted. Whether the conversion was a quick turn or a wide turn, it represented renouncing the old ways and surrendering to the Savior, Jesus. Their baptism marked a public identification with Jesus and with the community of those who followed him.

One of the consequences of conversion to become followers of Christ was the establishment of a new kind of home, one where Christ was Lord and that was in fellowship with other new Christian households. But we are not told what it was like for children brought up in such homes to confess Christ. Those second-generation Christians would want to affirm their environment, not renounce it, and the gospel would not be new—it would be something they'd heard from the time they were infants. To try to answer the question of the second generation (which can mean third- or fourth-generation, of course), Christians have sought wisdom from the teaching of the Old Testament, where there is great emphasis on the next generations. But there are also insights to be gained from the New Testament.

YOU MUST BE BORN AGAIN

Perhaps you are a concerned parent, and when you read the table of contents you spotted this chapter and turned here first. You need to go back and read the first part of the book, particularly my explanation of John 3:1–8. The starting point for any consideration of the spiritual life of our children is Jesus' categorical statement, "no one can see the kingdom of God unless he is born again." That must certainly include our children. The question is not, "Do our children need to be born again?" That is answered by Jesus. But in keeping with all of our discussion and case studies, the question is, "Will their *experience* of the new birth be different?" and the answer to that is most definitely yes. It will be different in that every person's experience is unique, but it will also be different because our children begin the process of coming to Christ from a very different starting point.

The birthline and the understanding of salvation as a process are particularly helpful in gaining insight into the new birth of our children. It helps us remember that the actual starting point of spiritual life is a mystery and can begin very early in a person's life if that is how God chooses to work. There is a reference to John the Baptist leaping in the womb of his mother in the presence of the unborn Christ (Luke 1:41). I wonder if that means we can say John was born again before he was born! This at least illustrates that spiritual life can begin very early in the life of a child. As we pray for our children, we should pray that the Spirit will begin to work while they are very young, even infants.

Throughout the history of the Christian church, the prayer of Christian parents that God will regenerate their children has often been linked to baptism ("unless he is born of water and the Spirit"). If you are not part of a tradition that baptizes children, you at least need to respect the sincere conviction that lies behind that practice. It is true, unfortunately, that in too many instances the water of baptism is given virtually magical powers to transform a child. For others, baptism of children is little more than a family celebration. However, there are also many examples of parents bringing their children to Christ as an act of faith to ask for his blessing on them. As they see the water applied outwardly, they trust that the Spirit will also be at work in their children's hearts.

Even if you do not express this trust through baptism, you can still believe that God will be at work in the life of your child. Be like those who brought their little children to Jesus so that he would lay his hands on them and bless them (Matt. 19:13–15). Note that Jesus was specifically speaking of these children when he said, "Let the little children come to me, and do not hinder them, *for the kingdom of heaven belongs to such as these.*" In an earlier incident (Matt. 18:1–4), Jesus used a child to illustrate the necessity of childlike faith, but in the incident of chapter 19 he is clearly referring to little children themselves. There are many interpretations of what Jesus meant when he spoke of the kingdom belonging to the little children, but we can at least conclude that the Lord welcomes our act of faith in bringing our children to him. It is difficult enough to raise children without adding the sense of responsibility of trying to do what *only* God can do. And he will do it! He has promised. This is when the Old Testament shines its light on the question of our children.

"I WILL BE YOUR GOD AND THE GOD OF YOUR CHILDREN"

One of the characteristics of God as he is revealed in the Bible is that he constantly enters into covenants with his people. God Almighty actually commits himself to be faithful and loyal to a people who again and again go their own way. Most of the time when God makes a covenant, he speaks of that covenant being passed along to the coming generations. He said to Abraham, "I will establish my covenant as an everlasting covenant between me and you *and your descendants* after you for the generations to come, to be your God and the God *of your descendants* after you" (Gen. 17:7).

I did not write this book to discuss all the aspects of theology relating to God's covenants. But as a practical matter, when we pray for our children and work with them in our homes and churches, the revelation of God's covenant-making and covenant-keeping should give us confidence that it is God's revealed intention to pass his salvation from generation to generation. The importance of this came home to me one day as I listened to a highly respected Christian leader talk about how he pleaded with God for the salvation of his children. On the one hand, it was very impressive to hear him speak of his heart for his children, but on the other hand there was a note of desperation in the way that he spoke about his concern. In the Presbyterian tradition, we use the expression *covenant children* to describe our children's unique standing before God. I believe that is a very helpful and biblical way to think of our children. We should pray with earnestness, but also with confidence that God will keep his promise.

Several months before I was married I was reading in Isaiah and came across this verse: "As for me, this is my covenant with them, saith the Lord; My spirit that is upon thee, and my words which I have put in thy mouth, shall not depart out of thy mouth, *nor out of the mouth of thy seed, nor out of the mouth of thy seed's seed,* saith the Lord, from henceforth and for ever" (59:21 kjv). That reference to future generations grabbed my attention, and in the margin of the Bible I was reading, I wrote "For Our Family" and added a date—"2/4/60." That was over a year before our wedding and more than two years before our first child was born, but I claimed that promise for the children and grandchildren who had not yet been born. I laid that Bible aside for years as I read other versions. When I was preparing to participate in the baptism of my first grandchild, I was drawn, for some reason, to pick up my old Bible and looked at this verse. I rediscovered my little note and the date, and I was overwhelmed with thanksgiving to realize that I was about to mark a very literal fulfillment of God's promise claimed thirty years earlier. Through tears of joy I said to the little gathering of believers, "God has kept his promise!"

This confidence in God's faithfulness is the most important single thing we can do for the salvation of our children. This does not in any way diminish our responsibility for their spiritual nurture, and in fact I think it frees us to do a more effective job. The lesson learned from the birthline—that we cannot cause spiritual birth, nor can we make the birth happen until it is ready—applies to our children as well. We trust God, but we are also willing to wait. Enjoy your children as gifts of God. Set about the challenging task of raising them, but do so in the confidence that *God loves our children.*

DO OUR CHILDREN NEED TO BE CONVERTED?

Our children are just as much in need of the new birth as all others. But if they are part of a family that is already following Jesus, what does it mean for them to *turn* (be converted) in order to follow Jesus? In a very real sense, they are already turned toward Christ. In a Christian home the head of the household says with Joshua, "But as for me *and my household, we* will serve the LORD" (Josh. 24:15). However, if we understand conversion as embracing Jesus Christ freely offered to us in the gospel, then certainly our children need to be converted.

What is difficult, in my observation both as a parent and a pastor, is that we aren't quite sure what sort of conversion experience to expect from our children. This seems to be especially challenging for parents who have come to faith out of a background of unbelief, even if theirs was a family that went to church. I have felt these parents to be much more anxious about the conversion of their children than parents who themselves were raised in strong Christian homes and who remember wrestling with the question of how to personally embrace the truths of the gospel that were part of their growing up.

In general, probably most of our children, growing up in evangelical families and evangelical churches where the language of conversion is so dominant, will have some memory of a conversion. Often they will pray the prayer to "ask Jesus into my heart" out of a sincere desire to please a parent or Sunday school teacher. That is not necessarily a bad thing, as in the case of Corrie ten Boom that I will relate. What I think is unfortunate and often confusing to our children is when we as parents or teachers view that childlike commitment as "the moment" and in effect put a mental check in the box we call *conversion*. We may find that our children pray a prayer for conversion any number of times as they go through the typical church experience of vacation Bible schools and church camps. They can come to wonder which time they prayed the prayer was when they "really meant it." When we are constantly evangelizing our children in this way, they can actually become hardened to the gospel because they think "I did that when I was seven."

Thinking of the process instead of dwelling on the issue of conversion is just as important for our children as it is for the other situations we have been discussing—perhaps even more important. Our children are growing up in the faith, and their young hearts are open to be taught the wonders of Scripture in story and song. Their young minds can memorize truth that will stay with them all of their lives. When this is absorbed by them in an environment of Christ's love and forgiveness displayed in our homes and churches, we are laying a foundation that will not be shaken. In earlier generations this was called "Christian nurture."

There are many valuable resources to help us in the Christian nurture of our children, but the most helpful is the Old Testament. Read Deuteronomy for its constant emphasis on thinking about the next generations, and notice that Proverbs is essentially a book of wisdom passed on from parents to children. One of the most significant insights for me as a young parent came through reflecting on the Ten Commandments (Ex. 20; Deut. 5). It occurred to me that *before* he spoke the Law, the Lord assured his people of his unconditional love: "I am the LORD your God, who brought you out of Egypt, out of the land of slavery." His relationship was the foundation for the law that followed. And it was stated in very basic words, with the clear understanding that it would be enforced. It became my prayer that my children would always know of my unconditional love, but they would also know that because I loved them, I would expect obedience.

THE CONVERSION OF CORRIE TEN BOOM

One of the most admired Christians of the twentieth century was Corrie ten Boom. She and her family courageously hid Jews from the Nazis when Holland was occupied during World War II. Corrie told this story in her book *The Hiding Place*. In the decades following the war, God used Corrie to challenge countless believers to sacrificially follow Christ. That included an unforgettable visit to the congregation I was pastoring in Washington, DC.

In a book about her family, Corrie wrote, "I loved stories, particularly those about Jesus. He was a member of the ten Boom family—it was just as easy to talk to Him as it was to carry on a conversation with my mother and father, my aunts, or my brother and sisters. He was there."[2]

Corrie's conversion took place at a young age when her mother noticed her pretending to knock on a door as she played house. Her mother told Corrie that she knew someone was knocking at her own door right then. Corrie wrote:

> I know now that there was a preparation within my childish heart for that moment; the Holy Spirit makes us ready for acceptance of Jesus Christ, of turning our life over to Him.
>
> "Jesus said that He is standing at the door, and if you invite Him in He will come into your heart," my mother continued. "Would you like to invite Jesus in?"
>
> At that moment my mother was the most beautiful person in the whole world to me.
>
> "Yes, Mama, I want Jesus in my heart."
>
> So she took my little hand in hers and we prayed together. It was so simple, and yet Jesus Christ says that we all must come as children, no matter what our age, social standing, or intellectual background.
>
> When Mother told me later about this experience, I recalled it clearly.

2. Corrie ten Boom, *In My Father's House* (Old Tappan, NJ: Fleming H. Revell, Guideposts Edition, 1976), 25.

> Does a child of five really know what he's doing? Some people say that children don't have spiritual understanding—that we should wait until a child can "make up his mind for himself." I believe a child should be led, not left to wander.[3]

That is a beautiful story of a childlike step of faith. Note that Corrie comments that the Spirit prepared her for that moment (and perhaps also gave her mother the discernment that it was the right time to speak to her child). When Corrie mentions that her mother told her later about the incident, it makes me think that for Corrie her simple prayer was just one piece of growing up in a home where "Jesus was a member of the ten Boom family." Even in this brief excerpt it is clear that the commitment was made in a home filled with the love of Christ. The book from which the quotation was taken tells the story of a godly Dutch Reformed home, where the spiritual stamina and character were formed that prepared them all for the extraordinary ministry described in *The Hiding Place*.

But if Corrie ten Boom represents those children who remember a time of commitment, I know of many committed adult Christians who grew up in such an environment and cannot remember a time when they weren't trusting in Christ. In many evangelical circles it is unacceptable to describe one's spiritual life that way, and when the only testimonies heard are about dramatic conversions, our children can actually begin to doubt the reality of their salvation. When I talk about this issue in classes and seminars, I regularly get expressions of appreciation from those who have no recollection of a conversion. Many have said they grew up feeling like a second-class Christian, even though there was a deep conviction that they were trusting only in Christ.

3. Ibid., 26–27.

In one of my classes a Korean student, who is now a pastor, found this insight particularly helpful. He told us that he grew up in a godly and loving home, but that for years he prayed that God would *take away* his faith so he could become an unbeliever; then he could get converted and become a "real" Christian. We need to think carefully about the messages we are sending to our children.

At some point in the process there needs to be an opportunity for our children to publicly profess Christ as Lord and Savior. In most cases that will take the form of a ceremony of admission to full membership in a church and the taking of the Lord's Supper (including baptism for those who do not baptize children). There are many variations of this pattern, but my point here is to emphasize the importance of such a ceremony as a marker along the path of our children's spiritual journey. They need a point they can look back to and remember when they stood up and acknowledged publicly that they were trusting in Christ alone for salvation in a way that is tied to their association with a Christian community. This should come when they are old enough to receive instruction in the faith and when they can be reflective enough to decide if they are ready to make such a confession. When a child postpones taking this step, it can be agonizing for parents who want to see their children fully embrace Christ, but merely going through a ceremony for the sake of appearance is not helpful. On the other hand, waiting for children to be able to describe a defining conversion moment puts the emphasis back on experience. If they are willing to receive instruction and then publicly confess Christ before the church, we should welcome them into the fellowship.

It should go without saying that I am describing a general pattern. This is consistent with what we have been saying throughout our study of the new birth, and we can expect to hear the same kinds of different experiences in children from Christian families. Some will report that they never moved from the path and never had what some consider a mandatory time of rebellion. Others will describe going through seasons of little perceptible growth or times of doubting, but they would inevitably be drawn back to the spiritual life that was theirs from the beginning. Even those who go through a time of serious rebellion, like the prodigal son, usually speak of their return more as coming home than as a conversion out of unbelief.

Sadly, there are also stories of prodigals who never come home. There are many examples of those who grow up in Christian homes but end up turning away from the faith they were taught as children. We look for ways to find fault with the parents or bad church experiences, and we resolve not to let that be repeated in our situations. But the reasons why people leave the faith of their parents are not always obvious. Furthermore, any of us whose children have believed can point to many weaknesses on our parts. We know our children didn't come to faith because we were such perfect parents or because our churches did everything right. In the end we seek to be faithful, but we also simply must humbly trust in God whose work is mysterious, like the blowing of the wind.

THE SPIRITUAL JOURNEYS OF THE CHILDREN OF STEVE AND SANDY SMALLMAN

Sandy and I have four adult children who have all professed Christ and have married Christian spouses. We are profoundly grateful to God for this gift. I asked each of them to reflect on the birthline and then write an account of their own spiritual journeys. Here are the stories (abbreviated) of four children raised in the same Christian home and the same church but with four different stories to tell:

Steve Smallman Jr.

I was raised in a Christian home. My father is a pastor, and Mom was always an integral part of the ministry of the church. In this church, I feel that we were well taught. We were taught the stories of the Bible and their meaning. Similarly, it would be difficult to overestimate the overall impact of the climate of our home on my spiritual development. But for me, this was not dramatic or traumatic. It may not make for good storytelling, but it was the floor beneath my feet. My parents taught us and lived the Christian life in front of us.

In my case, I just accepted this as truth. I do not ever remember feeling otherwise. I never experienced a season of unbelief. Even in times of doubt or uncertainty, I sought answers to my questions because my heart was searching for the way home. I don't think I was ever looking for a different spiritual base. So when God used different life experiences to bring profound change or greater obedience, awakening or deepened love for him, these events all just pointed back to what my heart had always known. It was usually a return to "the Jesus I *always* knew."

I can remember attending a Christian father and son ministry as a child. These meetings were run by folks who held that the conversion event, that defining moment when one "accepts Jesus as personal Lord and Savior," is of prime importance. I can remember being aware that I did not have such an experience. Their definition of a "testimony" was the story of that time when you "accepted Jesus" by praying the sinner's prayer or going forward at a revival meeting. Since I could not recall an experience like this, I didn't know what to say when it was time for me to give my "testimony." *So I just made one up.* This was not a crisis of faith. I think even at that early age I had an inward sense of who I was. I didn't conclude that I wasn't a Christian, just that I didn't have a good "testimony." I felt like I belonged with other Christian kids. I don't ever remember feeling phony or out of place.

When I was nineteen and home for the summer from my first year of college, I was living the life of any self-absorbed young adult. I enjoyed partying with friends, staying out late and living as I pleased. I wasn't rebelling against anybody or trying to hurt anyone. Since this wasn't my intent, I thought I couldn't be blamed for the impact my life was having on my own family and others. I hadn't been arrested or caused the family any traumatic shame, but I also wasn't moving forward in any real way and was becoming a burden to my parents who had to have my life in their face every day. A major season of awakening to Christ's love began when a minor household conflict led my father to voice some concerns that had been growing in his mind for a number of months. He did this in writing so as to measure his words and give me opportunity to reflect on them. The result of the letter he wrote was that I saw myself as a sinner. While I'd always heard that and knew it to be true (I had been caught in wrongdoing before and disciplined accordingly many times), I don't think I had assessed the reality of it quite so profoundly as I did after reading that letter. I saw that I had failed some people whose approval I valued. I also saw that my conduct amounted to a failure to honor God. I remember experiencing an immediate desire to repent, and there were outward signs of it virtually overnight. I now desired to please my parents and God, and this *level* of desiring was something new to me. I now believe that God gave me this desire to prepare me. Over the course of that summer God began to reveal to me, through a series of experiences, my profound spiritual bankruptcy and my real need for him to run my life. He began to show me some of the consequences of my actions, consequences that couldn't be undone by a desire to please him or live better. Was this my conversion? Possibly. But I have conscious recollection of my heart being warmed by sermons, songs, Christian fellowship, and the presence of God years before this time.

As a pastor now myself, this way of viewing not just spiritual birth and conversion but all of the spiritual life has really become a paradigm. For me, it is an acknowledgment of God's ultimate control of the "flow." It's what an older woman in our church used to say: "Hang loose with the Lord." You just have to roll with it, let God do his thing in his time in his way. We just have to show up. I'm very comfortable with this, and it just makes sense to me from my study of the Scriptures and from looking back over my own life.

Cynthia Smallman DelVecchio

I would have to say that I have no memory of a time when I *didn't* have a relationship with God in some form. When you are raised hearing about God and the work of Christ essentially from birth, it's difficult to see a "before and after." I definitely remember praying "the prayer" when I was in about second grade. I'm not sure if this was because of a conviction of sin on the part of the Holy Spirit, or just me feeling the pressure to do something that I knew was expected of me (perhaps a little of both). I know that I didn't feel any different after "becoming a Christian," and this caused me a great deal of confusion as I continued on my spiritual journey. For a long time I thought that I must not really be a Christian since

I hadn't had a radical conversion experience. I prayed "the prayer" silently to myself on many occasions to make sure I really was a Christian. The turning point came for me at a youth camp (around age fourteen) when I had a conversation with our associate pastor's wife and confessed to her my frustration over never really "feeling" like a Christian. She said to me, "Cindy, I think you're looking for an experience instead of looking for Christ." From that point on my perspective definitely changed. I really knew that I was a Christian and that I needed to pursue Christ instead of waiting for something incredible to happen that would give me an awesome testimony.

I have thought a lot about how we want to present Christ to our kids. We have purposely not talked a lot about them becoming Christians and have definitely not asked them if they want to "accept Jesus into their hearts." Our two elder daughters have "prayed the prayer," but I'm not sure what prompted them to do it. Our attitude is more that we assume a relationship with God on their parts and try to nurture that in any way that we see fit, through regular church and youth group attendance, encouraging their participation in small groups led by other adults, family Bible reading and prayer times, exposure to a wide variety of other Christians, and certainly as much open discussion as possible about how to live Christianly in a very evil world. At some point I believe they will come to a crossroads in their lives where they will decide what they are going to believe and how they will live. By God's grace we hope they ultimately will decide to try to live as godly women. While we certainly have made and will make many mistakes in our parenting, I think that our kids will know without question that Christ is the cornerstone of our lives and that we rely on him for daily sustenance, just as I saw that modeled by my own parents.

Christa Smallman Sutherland

I am a first-rate church brat. I have never known life outside of a Christian community. I can't remember my first church service, my first prayer, my first hymn. It has always been a part of my life. The church building itself seemed simply an extension of our home. I loved workdays and potlucks and, of course, church picnics.

If one were to ask me when I was "spiritually conceived," I couldn't answer. Perhaps the spiritual conception was there even before I was physically born. However, one of my more significant memories of church was when I was about seven years old. One Sunday afternoon I stormed rather noisily into the house after playing outside. My father was in the living room with one of the elders of our church. He said something to the effect of, "Christa, we were just about to pray for our evening service tonight. We are hoping that someone will accept Jesus as their Savior. Would you care to join us?" I said I would, and the three of us prayed. From that time until the service that night I felt a new and inward gnawing in my heart. Years later as I was joining the church I remember learning the term *effectual calling*. It was then that I understood what I had felt that afternoon.

I can't recount one word that was said during that evening service, but I do remember walking to the front of the church in my purple polyester pantsuit with the vest twisted up in the back and giving my life to Jesus. (Someone fixed the vest for me. After all, how can you have someone newly converted with a twisted up vest!) We went to McDonald's that night, and a woman from our church gave me a little booklet of the Gospel of John and encouraged me to read the Bible every day. I remember not quite knowing how to act. Was it OK to be silly? Could I goof around with my friends? I couldn't explain all that had taken place that day, but I felt that I was a different person from the seven-year-old girl who woke up that morning.

I lived happily ever after as an obedient Christian girl. Not hardly! Knowing much about God and about spiritual truths and even having a "conversion experience" did not make the world any less alluring. We grew up in an upper-middle-class suburb of Washington, DC. All around me was wealth and accomplishment. The people were "beautiful" people in every sense of the word. They were smart, important, and wealthy. During junior high and high school I desperately longed for that in my own life. God in his grace and infinite mercy gave me none of these things. I was insecure, unpopular, and broke! Many of my classmates were daughters or sons of someone famous—my father was just a pastor. I was a selfish girl willing to be obedient only if it meant getting what I wanted when I wanted it. How dare God plan my life according to his will and not my own! By the end of my high school years I was really angry. I remember crying out in my room one night, "I hate you, God, I hate you!" Consumed by my own selfish desires, my faith was in peril.

I am a rather dramatic person (my family has used the term *hysterical*). I wanted God to strike me with lightning. He would not do it. He did, however, draw me again to himself in a still, small voice. After my honest encounter with God, I decided very logically to be obedient. I never doubted that God was in control, but I was not convinced that he was good. I basically thought, *OK, if God wants me to live life as a thoroughly boring person with nothing to offer, then that's what I need to do*. That's about the best I could do at that time. But God took my measly offering and began, once again, to turn my heart toward him. I finally had a new joy and peace that I had not had through junior and senior high school, and I slowly began to believe again in the goodness of God. Through my last painful year

175

of high school, the church became a haven for me. Sundays replenished me in a new way, and in particular the loving care and concern of men and women in our church family enveloped me and lifted my spirits. I am forever grateful for their genuine love for me and my family. My faith would not have survived without them.

How do I explain my spiritual pilgrimage? When was I "truly" converted? Was it at age seven or as a high school senior? Has it been one of the many occasions since that have challenged my faith and caused me to once again fall on my knees before the Lord? This is what I believe to be the unique nature of growing up in the nurture and admonition of the Lord. There has never been an escape from the deep spiritual truths I have known. And yet knowing has not equated into living those same truths. The grace in my life has not been God making himself known to me because in one sense I have always known him. The grace has come in his continuing to reveal himself to me and continuing to draw me to himself when many times he should have thrown up his hands in disgust! The great sin in my life has not been drugs or alcohol or an unplanned pregnancy. The great sin has been far worse! It has been knowing the truth and then turning away. It has been, in essence, throwing in God's face all the spiritual riches he has lavished on me since I was born.

Will Smallman

It's hard for me to describe my conversion experience, because in many ways I feel I've converted numerous times, and these experiences have taken many different forms. I remember, as a child of maybe ten years old, sitting upright in bed, suddenly terrified as I was struck by the notion that I might go to hell. That night I converted out of fear for my soul, out of a panic-driven need to avoid eternal damnation. There was the night

176

in Chile, as an eighteen-year-old, that I was made painfully aware of my own total lack of faith and my great vanity and decided to rededicate myself to a life of faith, though just what that life of faith was supposed to entail, I wasn't sure.

Finally, there was the night (these experiences always occurred at night, which makes me think of Hemingway's line in *The Sun Also Rises:* "It is awfully easy to be hard-boiled about everything in the daytime, but at night it is another thing") in college when, after a prolonged period of frustration and anxiety I once again recommitted my life to Christ, reasoning in a somewhat pragmatic fashion that as I had absolutely no control over myself or the circumstances of my life, God must be in control, and I therefore had no choice but to rededicate my life to him. In essence, I converted this time because I no longer had any hope in anything else.

Unfortunately, after each of these experiences I would begin to feel a sense of frustration and loss in equal proportion to the zeal with which I converted as I sensed that nothing had really changed. I would still fear the fires of hell, still be consumed by insurmountable pride and vanity, still walk the streets with a sense of fear and anxiety. Most importantly I would still doubt.

These experiences weren't irrelevant, however, and the mere fact that I remember a few of them so vividly suggests to me that they were significant in some way. They weren't what I was searching for, and for that reason they were disappointing, but they weren't irrelevant either. I was waiting and hoping, all through my childhood and teen years, for a breakthrough experience that would change everything, waiting for that one night when I would burst through the clouds of my doubt and fear and would soar to the heavens on a magic carpet of faith and understanding, trailing tears in my wake. I had heard about these experiences before, in Sunday school classes and church gatherings. Somebody, typically a middle-aged man, would stand humbly in the front of the room and speak with remorse about his days as a drug-, sex-, and alcohol-addicted neo-Nazi and how, on one rain-soaked night, he pulled off the highway in his stolen car and wept, begging Christ for forgiveness. This would be the night that changed everything, the night that catapulted him from a life of sin to a life of sublime faith.

Of course, I would never have such an experience. Pastors' sons who grew up in split-level suburban homes would never be able to feel the joy of a true conversion, not when they had been raised in a perfect nuclear family, with a dog, loving parents, and aluminum siding to ensure them a safe and happy childhood. But I tried anyway and ultimately was left disappointed and disillusioned when my life didn't take an abrupt left turn after a night of sincere recommitment. Looking back, however, I see that each of these experiences serves as a kind of milepost, marking the slow progress of my faith through the years, and they demonstrate God's unyielding hold on my life. These moments, despite the disappointment that followed them, were moments in which I genuinely felt the call of God. Each time I would fail to heed that call, but eventually he would call me back.

What I realized in college, and what I haven't forgotten, is that my own personal failings will never truly distance me from God. I will doubt, and I will rant, and I will swell with pride and be crippled by vanity, but ultimately God will call me back, and I will have to respond. What I no longer search for is a sense of finality in these moments, a sense that one night or one experience will prevent me from future struggle and frustration in my attempts to live by faith.

This is as close as I can come to explaining my conversion. I don't remember the first time I prayed *the* prayer or the first time I understood what salvation meant. I was born and raised a Christian, and those moments I described are as close as I can come to establishing a sense of how I arrived at the beliefs I hold now. At least now I can take comfort in the knowledge that God will continue to call me, regardless of the great personal failings that seem to cripple my every attempt at a life of faith.

CHAPTER 14

Living for the King

IT IS FITTING THAT WE END the book at the place it began, with the conversation between Jesus and Nicodemus about the new birth. Consider again the statement Jesus made to Nicodemus: "I tell you the truth, no one can see the kingdom of God unless he is born again" (John 3:3). We have looked carefully at the new birth as a work of the Holy Spirit in the individual and have tried to gain insight into what it looks like in actual experience. But it would be an unfortunate oversight if we neglected the fact that Jesus was quite emphatic that being born again, or born from above, was the entry point into *the kingdom of God*. He repeated this thought as he began to explain more about the new birth: "I tell you the truth, no one can enter *the kingdom of God* unless he is born of water and the Spirit" (v. 5).

We read in John 3 that Nicodemus was surprised by Jesus' answer, but that doesn't mean he was surprised to hear Jesus speak of the kingdom of God. No doubt that was what caused him to seek out Jesus. The coming of the kingdom was what both John the Baptist and Jesus had been announcing. In the context of the Old Testament promises, *that is the gospel*—the good news that God has actually come to reign on the earth (Isa. 52:7–10; Luke 2:10–11, 29–32). After centuries of waiting for the promised age of justice and righteousness, the peaceable kingdom had arrived. No wonder the Jewish people gathered in great numbers to hear whether there was any substance to what these preachers had to say. And when Jesus backed up his announcement with actual miracles, Nicodemus was impressed and wanted to find out more.

I am not sure that Nicodemus came to Jesus expecting to be told about personal spiritual birth, but that is what he needed to hear. That was the right place to start for Nicodemus, and it is the right place to start today. But if we are to carry out ministry in line with Jesus' teaching, we need to view the new birth as a doorway into something far greater—the kingdom of God. *My challenge to all who are working with others is to ask how central this great truth of the kingdom is to us personally and to the way we do ministry.* If we are to do an effective job as spiritual midwives who are making disciples, we need to include an awareness of the kingdom right from the start of our ministries with people.

It should be expected that people who come to Christ will be preoccupied with their own needs. To be a sinner means to be self-centered. Then, as the Spirit works, people are made aware of their sin and the frightful prospect of standing before God; there is a dawning awareness of how little they know of Christ; and finally, they struggle to know what it means to believe in him. This means that people come into the kingdom still very self-centered, just like babies at the time of delivery. That may be normal, but it needs to change.

WHAT IS THE KINGDOM OF GOD?

We talk about "seeking first the kingdom" or "working for the kingdom," but what does all that mean? The kingdom is essentially the rule of God on earth through his King, the Lord Jesus Christ. We experience the kingdom here on earth, but it is spiritual. By the inward, transforming work of the Spirit we enter into the realm of God's saving power, which Jesus came to earth to establish. In one sense the kingdom *has come* in the coming of Jesus himself. But because of the foundation that Jesus laid through his death, resurrection, and ascension, the kingdom *is now coming* through the power of the Holy Spirit that Jesus poured out on his church once he ascended to the Father. The church that Jesus is building is actually the visible sign of the invisible kingdom. And finally the kingdom *will come* in all of its majesty at some point in the future. Theologians tell us that we are living today in the *already, but not yet* phase of the kingdom.

A more detailed discussion of the kingdom is beyond the scope of this book. I hope these few thoughts will encourage additional reading and discussion of this topic. Don't think of this only as a biblical or theological issue that any well-informed Christian should know about. I encourage such study as a practical matter of how we go about ministry.

FROM CHRISTIAN LIVING TO LIVING FOR THE KING

In my own pilgrimage, a new appreciation of the kingdom came about through a rediscovery of the Lord's Prayer. Out of deep dissatisfaction with my own prayer life many years ago, I began to use the prayer Jesus gave his disciples as an outline for my daily prayers. What started as an experiment in learning to pray continues to this very day. I simply pray each phrase and then expand its meaning. This brings me immediately into God's presence as my *Father*. Because of Jesus, I can address God Almighty with the same intimacy he did. As I speak to my Father in heaven I'm first prompted to worship and pray for the honor of his name. Then I pray, "your kingdom come." Those are high-sounding words, but before long I began to wrestle with what I was praying for when I prayed for God's kingdom to come. It certainly meant prayer for the *fulfillment* of the kingdom and the return of Christ. (Until learning to pray through the Lord's Prayer, I confess I seldom prayed for these things.) But it meant more than that. Reflecting on the aspects of the kingdom I just described, it meant praying that my life personally would embody the centrality of Jesus the King, who *has come* to bring the kingdom. Furthermore, in that the kingdom *is now coming*, it was a challenge to pray for the work of the kingdom going on through Jesus' church and the preaching of the gospel all over the world. I soon realized that the accompanying phrase, "your will be done on earth as it is in heaven" is not a separate petition but a definition of the kingdom. What we are longing for as we pray is that the perfect rule of Christ that is true in God's presence (heaven) will also be true in some measure in our lives and here on earth.

Praying consistently "your kingdom come, your will be done on earth as it is in heaven" means we are praying for at least three things:

1. The renewal of our devotion to Christ our King. In the language of older Christian spirituality, we are finding our *center* in Jesus.

2. The mission of Jesus. That is not only the work of the gospel but the coming of peace to a broken world. It is a prayer for peace and justice in society as well as personally.

3. The return of Jesus. "Come Lord Jesus." We long for that day when "the earth will be covered with the knowledge of the LORD as the waters cover the sea" (Isa. 11:9).

As we pray for the kingdom to come, we will see God answer, in part, by what he does in our own lives. I have seen a real change in how I view living my life in Christ. It is the Christian life, to be sure, but I think a better description is to call it "living for the King." As the importance of the kingdom kept growing in my understanding, I actually developed a discipleship program for our church by that name.

There is an important point here in terms of the purpose of this book. Jesus, who told Nicodemus about the new birth as the entrance to the kingdom of God, also taught this kingdom-focused prayer to his disciples as a *beginner's prayer*. His disciples were taught from the beginning about the kingdom. If we are obeying his command to "make disciples," we should be doing the same. It may take a while to understand what that means, as it did Jesus' earliest disciples (Acts 1:1–8), but a kingdom perspective needs to be part of discipleship even before conversion.

In explaining salvation to the new believers in Colossae, Paul taught them that God "has rescued us from the dominion of darkness and brought us into the *kingdom of the Son he loves*, in whom we have redemption, the forgiveness of sins" (Col. 1:13–14). Paul then taught that the salvation they experienced was a taste of God's greater redemption when God would "reconcile to himself *all things, whether things on earth or things in heaven*, by making peace through his blood, shed on the cross" (vv. 19–22). A kingdom perspective was not only a lesson for mature believers; it was part of Paul's *first* teaching, as it was for Jesus. Discipleship that keeps reinforcing the individualistic approach to the Christian life, defining the spiritual life almost entirely in terms of a personal relationship with Jesus, will miss this. We need to open people's spiritual eyes to help them see what they have entered through the new birth.[1]

FIXING OUR EYES ON JESUS
WHO IS SEATED ON THE THRONE

Imagine a tunnel with a little glimmer of light at the end. You move slowly toward the end and see more and more of the light, even though you are still in darkness. Finally you pass out of the tunnel only to find out that it is really a doorway into a great stadium filled with cheering fans. At first you are blinded by the light, but soon you move onto the field of play to run your race, and you find out that all those fans are cheering for *you*. And on the field you discover the smiling face of Jesus, waiting for you. He knows you, and you somehow know him and realize that it was his

---

1. I encourage those involved in a discipleship ministry to consider the Lord's Prayer as a primary resource. We far too easily overlook the obvious in looking for materials to teach. Begin teaching it as a memorized prayer, but then use it to teach on the elements of Christian living suggested by each phrase.

kindness that got you to the field, and now he is there to encourage you on.

This is another way to describe the process of the new birth and the life that follows. It is a life begun in darkness, but through the work of Jesus and the inner call of the Spirit we step into a new life. What started as a solitary journey ends with our being a part of something greater than we ever dreamed of—we have entered the kingdom of God. We have a personal story, but now we are part of the ongoing story of God's plan to bring the whole world under the gracious rule of King Jesus. What an extraordinary privilege! And what a privilege to be part of that unfolding story in the lives of others!

> Therefore, since we are surrounded by such a great cloud of witnesses, let us throw off everything that hinders and the sin that so easily entangles, and let us run with perseverance the race marked out for us. Let us fix our eyes on Jesus, the author and perfecter of our faith, who for the joy set before him endured the cross, scorning its shame, and sat down at the right hand of the throne of God. Consider him who endured such opposition from sinful men, so that you will not grow weary and lose heart. . . .
>
> Therefore, since we are receiving a kingdom that cannot be shaken, let us be thankful, and so worship God acceptably with reverence and awe, for our "God is a consuming fire." (Heb. 12:1–2, 28–29)

Beginnings and African-American Culture

BEING AN AFRICAN-AMERICAN church planter who grew up in the black Baptist church and currently serves as a pastor in the inner city, I have noticed some theological deficits and unfortunate trends that have plagued African-American Christian culture for years. While all cultures have unique tendencies that move people away from biblical doctrines, I have become all too familiar with the divorce between discipleship and evangelism in African-American theology. I have many memories of evangelists and pastors at churches when I was growing up who called for people to "profess Christ" or "repeat this prayer" yet were not actively involved discipling anyone. Many of the individuals I pastor either struggle with insecurity because they *do* believe the gospel, yet they cannot recall a specific moment where they were converted, or they are not walking with God but they claim that they know they are saved because they walked forward at an altar call as a child. The unfortunate emphasis of evangelism over discipleship has left generations of believers and unbelievers confused and discouraged. *Beginnings* has been a breath of fresh air for my congregation and me, as we have systematically discovered how Jesus was not only concerned about evangelism, but discipleship. What is more, true discipleship does not wait for a profession of faith, but instead, it can begin when meeting a person and it encompasses that person's whole life.

When I first decided to read *Beginnings*, then titled *Spiritual Birthline*, my purpose was to try to connect the dots between evangelism and discipleship in the African-American culture. The book is biblically sound, and Pastor Smallman utilizes a theological lens that shows discipleship as a process that both magnifies God and missionally engages unbelievers. As a Reformed pastor, I wanted the doctrines of grace to inform my discipleship as well as to provide answers for those in my congregation who had been damaged by the church. I was becoming more aware that so many young people have "testimony envy," wishing that they had a spectacular conversion story that both settled their own fears and convinced others of their standing with God. I was also interacting with more and more people who clearly were not walking with the Lord, yet who had a firm confidence in their salvation. It seemed that the evangelist's efforts of prior generations, while done with good intentions, had ultimately given more questions than answers, and people were clueless when it came to such an important command as "making disciples."

As I've already implied, we cannot evaluate the present until we properly understand the past, and taking a close look at what the African-American church in the last century has looked like is ultimately the key to answering questions about discipleship today. Throughout my childhood and adolescence I remember the great emphasis at church was "getting saved." The pastor showed his concern with salvation by frequently having altar calls during his sermons where he would do his best to convince people to come to the front of the church to repeat a prayer or "ask Jesus into your heart." The pastor wasn't alone; we were all given the responsibility to witness to as many people as possible in order to have a large tally of "professions." We did this by hitting the streets and handing out tracts, most of which were filled with horrifying cartoon images and fictional narratives of people who were now in hell. In fact, getting people to accept Christ in order to escape hell was the ultimate, if not the only, goal in our evangelism. This mind-set stayed with me in the early days of my ministry; however, as I read the text of Scripture more, I began to see that the great commission was not a call to evangelism, but to discipleship.

My perspective has changed. I realized that some people do have radical conversion stories and some people don't, and both are OK. However, we should not let the experience of some people define the expected experience of others. An unfortunate result of this overemphasis of evangelism is the fact that many pastors and laypeople alike do not want to waste their time with unbelievers. In fact, many pastors today don't want to talk about anything with unbelievers except salvation. Once those people gets saved, they are willing to invest in their lives and build relationships, but until then there can only be discussions on salvation.

Beginnings has really helped me confront that reality as it showed me that God is ultimately responsible for salvation and often works through long processes. As I like to say, *we need a Crock-Pot ministry, not a frying pan ministry*. Many people need to be slow-cooked, and we need to take our time with them in the same way that God does. As pastors, we need to be fishers of men, not hunters of men. We need to use fishing rods with lures, not harpoons. Unfortunately, our culture likes quick results and our impatience is evident in everything we do.

If someone wants to have a beautiful front lawn, he will probably buy sod if he can afford it. Why waste time waiting for grass to grow from a seed? This mentality has informed the way we do ministry. We want someone to say a prayer or make a profession so that we can have "sod Christians." We are unwilling to plant the seed and do what we should to help it grow so that it can one day sprout into grass. We are unwilling to spend time with unsaved people because we believe that we cannot disciple them until they are saved, but this is simply not the case. Discipleship is a process that can begin the moment you meet someone. In John 6:66, we see that many who were following Jesus turned away and left him. These people were following and learning from Jesus, but they left, and apparently they were not regenerate individuals. However, it seems that they still functioned as disciples of Christ. In the same way that Jesus invested his time into people who did not believe in him, we are called to do the same. We must recognize that Jesus is already the Master before people accept him. Jesus called people to lose their lives, not "get saved." Jesus never asked people to simply complete one act or prayer in order to escape hell; he ultimately called them to a new life that began when they met him. Jesus tells people to *follow him* and *learn from him*, which is a reference to ongoing discipleship. The misguided preacher wants a "profession," but Jesus wants a life.

Since applying the concepts in *Beginnings* to our ministry, the elders and I have made a great deal of progress in our young church plant. In the city of Camden, many people either hate church or have never been to church. It was unrealistic for me to believe that people would be converting left and right (though that is possible and would have been great). I realized that I would have to invest in people's lives for a long time, and I would have to be a discipler, not just an evangelist (2 Tim. 4:5).

One of the first people I met when moving to Camden was a drug dealer potentially facing a twenty-year jail term. The elders and I quickly befriended him and we all began to spend a lot of time together. The gentleman would come to church and he didn't mind hearing us talk about Jesus. On various occasions I asked him if was interested in becoming a true follower of Christ, and for two years he respectfully declined. An old criminal charge came to light and Buck was incarcerated for thirteen months. The leadership and I wrote him letters often and continued to invest in our friendship with him. One day he mentioned that he was leading a Bible study, and he followed up that story with news that he was now a Christian. I shared the news with our congregation and they celebrated, and this past year I had the privilege of baptizing him. For two years I discipled Buck, even though he was not a Christian. If I had done nothing but prod him about his salvation, we would not have remained friends for very long. Instead, I loved him, prayed for him, and showed him the truth of Christianity, and God in his sovereignty was pleased to save Buck one day in jail. *Beginnings* not only informed my interactions with Buck, but it has also affected the way our entire covenant community participates in ministry. First, the application of the book has increased our effectiveness as ministers of the gospel. Second, it reduces the stress and pressure of trying to convince people to convert, because it puts God in place a sovereign king. Lastly, it helps us to glorify God more in our ministry, because it magnifies him as the ultimate Converter and Redeemer.

DOUGLAS A. LOGAN JR.

PHYSICAL AND SPIRITUAL BIRTH

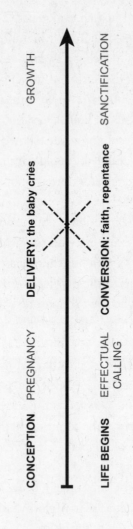

Physical birth

CONCEPTION — PREGNANCY — DELIVERY: the baby cries — GROWTH

LIFE BEGINS — EFFECTUAL CALLING — CONVERSION: faith, repentance — SANCTIFICATION

Spiritual birth—*regeneration*

A Class on the Birthline and Related Matters

THE FOLLOWING is a suggested outline for a six-week class that will take students through *Beginnings* and incorporates assignments mentioned in the book. The format requires an instructor who has thoroughly digested the material in the book but includes presentations by members of the class and ample time for discussion. Six weeks is a typical modular class for Bible institutes and seminaries and assumes a full evening for the class and the readiness of the students to read and prepare assignments between classes.

A less intensive schedule of twelve weeks, such as a Sunday school class, would take two weeks to cover each of the classes. In such a class students should read the book, write their own autobiography, and be asked to talk to one other person about the birthline.

WEEK 1

Instruction and Discussion. The instructor should begin with a discussion of evangelism and discipleship in terms of the students' current understanding of those terms. This should anticipate some of the topics that will be raised in the book and the class. Move on to a careful study of John 3:1–8 and then an introduction of the birthline in a manner suggested at the end of chapter 3. The text of John 3 should be in front of the students, either in open Bibles or a copy of the passage. As students discuss the Scripture and the birthline, try to continually guide the discussion to make the students think about how it relates to their own experience, avoiding abstract theological discussions as much as possible.

Assignment. Read *Beginnings*, chapters 1–4.

Prepare the first draft of your spiritual autobiography as suggested in chapter 4.

WEEK 2

Instruction and Discussion. Review John 3:1–8, and discuss it in greater detail now that students have read the book. Review the particulars of the birthline. Make sure there is clarity about the definitions of the words used (chapter 2). Look at the content of chapter 4 and the two ideas of knowing and telling our stories. What are some of the dangers of testimonies?

Presentations. Invite students to tell their own stories in terms of the concepts presented in the birthline. They can be invited to read from their spiritual autobiographies, but this should not be required in that there may be some very personal information.

Give a significant amount of the class time for these presentations. The class should be encouraged to question and probe for greater understanding of the person's experience (anticipating the idea of a spiritual midwife). Rather than rushing though the presentations, reserve some for the next week.

Assignment. Read *Beginnings*, chapters 5–7.

Have all revise and rewrite their spiritual autobiography (not to be handed in).

WEEK 3

Instruction and Discussion. Discuss the material in chapters 5–6—the importance of Christian community for those coming to faith. What additional insights about the work of the Spirit come through the stories of Charles Colson and Tom Phillips? Move into the important issue of how the birthline relates to their working with others—the work of a spiritual midwife. Look carefully at the material in chapter 7, anticipating the assignment of case studies at the end of the class.

Presentations. Continue hearing the stories of the students.

Assignment. Read *Beginnings*, chapters 8–9.

Each student is to prepare three written case studies (one per week for the remaining three weeks of the class) to be handed in at the end of Week 6. Encourage the student to interview at least one person who did not have a dramatic conversion. The case studies should follow the simple format suggested in chapter 7:

1. Introduction

2. Narrative

3. Observations

WEEK 4

Instruction and Discussion. Study together the two passages in chapter 8 (1 Cor. 1:17—2:5 and 1 Thess. 1). Keep in mind that this is Paul's commentary on how the Spirit applies the gospel to the heart. Then look at the two conversions described in Acts. Discuss the material in chapter 9.

Presentations. Invite several students to present one of their case studies (these should be assigned the week before so those students will be sure to come prepared). Just as with the students' own stories, there should be time to allow the class to discuss and grow in understanding of the pilgrimage being presented.

Assignment. Read *Beginnings*, chapters 10–11.

Continue the preparation of case studies.

WEEK 5

Instruction and Discussion. Discuss the material in chapters 10 and 11. This is a very important presentation of calling and conversion. At this point students should be familiar with the terms, but now there is concentration on the actual experience. Refer back to the conversion of Malcolm X, mentioned in chapter 3, to help with the insight that Christians are not the only ones who experience conversion.

Presentations. Continue the presentation of case studies by students.

Assignment. Read *Beginnings*, chapters 12–14.

Complete work on case studies.

WEEK 6

Instruction and Discussion. The concluding chapters cover very important but diverse information. The discussion of the first steps of the new believer is really a discussion of the vitally important matter of discipleship and could be another class. Make sure to budget time for the discussion of the unique situation of children born in Christian homes. The issue of the kingdom of God is also important, but the chapter only serves to introduce the reader to the topic, and that is all that should be attempted in class.

Presentations. More presentations of case studies. It is unlikely that every case study can be presented and discussed in class. Make sure to leave time for a wrap-up discussion.

For Further Reading

Alexander, Archibald. *Thoughts on Religious Experience*. 1844. Reprint, London: Banner of Truth, 1967.

Barrs, Jerram. *The Heart of Evangelism*. Wheaton, IL: Crossway, 2001.

Fee, Gordon D. *Paul, the Spirit, and the People of God*. Peabody, MA: Hendrickson, 1996.

Ferguson, Sinclair. *The Christian Life: A Doctrinal Introduction*. Carlisle, PA: Banner of Truth Trust, 1989.

Metzger, Will. *Tell the Truth: The Whole Gospel Wholly by Grace Communicated Truthfully and Lovingly*. Downers Grove, IL: InterVarsity Press, 2012.

Miller, C. John. *A Faith Worth Sharing: A Lifetime of Conversations about Christ*. Phillipsburg, NJ: P&R Publishing, 1999.

Miller, Paul. *Love Walked among Us: Learning to Love Like Jesus*. Colorado Springs: NavPress, 2001.

Peace, Richard. *Conversion in the New Testament: Paul and the Twelve*. Grand Rapids: Eerdmans, 1999.

Petersen, Jim. *Lifestyle Discipleship: Encouraging Others to Spiritual Maturity*. Colorado Springs: NavPress, 1993.

Piper, John. *Finally Alive*. Fearn, Tain, Ross-Shire, Scotland; Christian Focus Publications, 2009.

Smallman, Stephen. *The Walk: Steps for New and Renewed Followers of Jesus*, Phillipsburg, NJ: P&R Publishing, 2009.

————. *What Is Discipleship?* Phillipsburg, NJ: P&R Publishing, 2011. [A booklet that grew out of my asking that question in chapter 12 on first steps of faith.]

————. *What Is True Conversion?* Phillipsburg, NJ: P&R Publishing, 2005. [A booklet for new believers; also useful in small groups; written to explore greater understanding of the new birth and how it is experienced.]

Smith, Gordon T. *Beginning Well: Christian Conversion and Authentic Transformation.* Downers Grove, IL: InterVarsity Press, 2001.

Wakabayashi, Allen Mitsuo. *Kingdom Come: How Jesus Wants to Change the World.* Downers Grove, IL: InterVarsity Press, 2003.

Webber, Robert E. *Ancient-Future Evangelism: Making Your Church a Faith-Forming Community.* Grand Rapids: Baker Books, 2003.

ADDITIONAL RESOURCES

Christianity Explored. Contact: www.christianityexplored.com. A ten-week program to introduce unbelievers to Christianity using the Gospel of Mark. Produced by All Souls Church of London.

SeeJesus.net. P.O. Box 197, Telford, PA 18969; www.seejesus.net. Small-group studies on the person of Jesus described in chapter 9. Designed by Paul Miller for those with little or no church.

Index of Scripture

203